Natural
Wonders
— *of* —
Michigan

Natural
Wonders
— *of* —
Michigan

A Guide to Parks, Preserves & Wild Places

Tom Carney

Illustrated by Lois Leonard Stock

Country Roads Press

CASTINE • MAINE

Natural Wonders of Michigan:
A Guide to Parks, Preserves & Wild Places

Published by Country Roads Press
P.O. Box 286, Lower Main Street
Castine, Maine 04421

Text and cover design by Studio 3, Ellsworth, Maine.
Cover photograph courtesy of Michigan Travel Bureau.
Illustrations by Lois Leonard Stock.
Typesetting by Typeworks, Belfast, Maine.

ISBN 1-56626-078-7

Library of Congress Cataloging-in-Publication Data

Carney, Tom.
    Natural wonders of Michigan : a guide to parks, preserves and
wild places / author, Tom Carney ; illustrator, Lois Leonard Stock.
        p.   cm.
    Includes index.
    ISBN 1-56626-078-7 : $9.95
    1. Michigan – Guidebooks.   2. Natural history – Michigan –
Guidebooks.   3. Natural places – Michigan – Guidebooks.
4. Parks – Michigan – Guidebooks.   5. Botanical gardens –
Michigan – Guidebooks.   I. Title.
F564.3.C37   1995
917.7404'43 – dc20   94-23590
                                                               CIP

Printed in the United States of America.
10 9 8 7 6 5 4 3 2 1

To my mother,
who has always guided well
through example

Contents

Acknowledgments

Thanks to Norris McDowell, the late Tom Anderson, and the late Al Stewart for their help in identifying spots to visit; also to the many people I've quoted in the various sections. If they've been quoted, then they were especially helpful. Special thanks also to Tom Huggler and to my wife, Maureen, each of whom continues to inspire in his or her special way.

Finally, to Clara Golenko of Rockport Shoes: my aching arches, throbbing knees, and sagging spirit thank you for the boots.

Introduction

It first made its presence known as we drove slowly one summer evening through the Pigeon River Country hoping to spy some elk. Then again, at high noon, as I peered across treetops growing from the Sinkholes. Most unexpectedly, it sang to us while we paused in the Seney Refuge. This phantom songbird enchanted with its varying, flutelike call though it eluded our view and left us with no field marks with which to confirm its identity.

Then, quite unexpectedly, the mystery was solved while I strolled through – of all places – the brand-new Logging Museum at Hartwick Pines. A special display matching the names of birds with their songs helped me out. The mascot for the journeys I had undertaken for this book was the hermit thrush.

Thus, experience coupled with serendipity produced discovery, which in turn reaffirmed an undeniable by-product of spending time in the outdoors: one's body of knowledge, elementary or not, only grows and grows. Wordsworth speaks of similar lessons in "The Tables Turned":

> *Up! up! my Friend, and quit your books;*
> *Or surely you'll grow double:*

Up! up! my Friend, and clear your looks;
Why all this toil and trouble? . . .
Books! 'tis a dull and endless strife:
Come, hear the woodland linnet,
How sweet his music! on my life,
There's more of wisdom in it. . . .
Come forth into the light of things,
Let Nature be your Teacher. . . .
Come forth, and bring with you a heart
That watches and receives.

I hope you receive as much from visiting the natural features in this guide as I did from writing about them.

USING THIS GUIDE

You are my guest. I am your host. Michigan is my home. Welcome.

Those four sentences represent the spirit in which I researched and prepared this guide.

There is no pretense that I have located for you the "best" places to visit. Nor will I even try to kid you into thinking that this is the "complete" guide to natural attractions in the state. Rather, what I offer are places I'd take you to if we were spending time together in any of five areas of Michigan.

As you might expect, I would take you to places that pass the muster of my own likes and dislikes, so you should know what those are before you join me.

I don't like being around lots of people. This is especially true when I'm trying to enjoy nature. And I don't mind rising extra early in order to visit places before the crowds arrive. I don't like to pay for the pleasure of experiencing nature; there's something incongruous about that concept. By the same token, I don't mind helping to defray the cost of developing and maintaining naturally appealing areas in a manner that makes them more accessible without destroying them. I've done my best to outgrow the zoo mentality that seems a part of our culture, and I don't want to perpetuate it by including places that exist primarily for the display of captive, nonnative species. A couple of other prejudices are so obvious I should admit them up front: Presque Isle and Marquette Counties in the Lower and Upper Peninsulas, respectively. Also, for this book, I want to emphasize nature's work and not man's. Therefore, with a few noteworthy exceptions, man takes a backseat in the pages that follow. Finally, the most popular attractions don't necessarily get the longest entries.

On the other hand, in *The Odyssey*, King Menelaus tells young Telemachus, "A host should not go too far in his likes or dislikes." Obviously, if I'm going to route you to places of natural splendor, I have to accept the fact that others, too, will be drawn to them. The best example of this is the entire section on northwestern Michigan. That area near Grand and Little Traverse Bays and the Leelanau Peninsula encompasses the most breathtaking landscapes in the Lower Peninsula. The Lake Michigan shoreline is a magnet for sunset watchers. The problem is that these landscapes and vistas have been cleaved into "real estate," and this part of the state is jammed with people, making it unsuitable when I seek solitude. So I compromised for that section. I included several attractions with the idea that they could be considered oases from the hordes of visitors who are concerned more with shopping, pleasure-boat cruising, and putt-putt golf than they are with exploring the wonders of the natural world.

TIPS FOR HIKERS

1. *Get comfortable hiking shoes.* Take it from one who learned through excruciating experience: if you plan to traverse any

number of trails, you'll appreciate a pair of light hiking shoes or boots instead of your basketball or boating shoes. Look for a comfortable fit, rigid support, and lug soles. It's a good idea to get a pair with a little room in the toes; this way, if you are heading downhill, your piggies will not get smushed against the front of the shoes. And you don't want Michigan's capricious weather messing up your plans. If you have rain gear so you can get outdoors in bad weather, be sure that your boots are waterproof too. Waterproofing will also help you remain comfortable if you hit the trails early in the morning when they are still soaked in dew. One of the easy-to-ignore benefits of waterproof boots comes the day after the rain. They will be dry and cozy, but a pair of canvas tennis shoes will most likely still be cold and clammy.

2. *Protect against insects*. Vacation time in Michigan, June through August, is also the height of biting-bug season. Even if you are taking only a ten-minute sashay through a local Metropark, you'll be glad you decided to spray on some repellent before leaving. And don't forget to take appropriate precautions against deer ticks, which carry Lyme disease. Such precautions include donning caps, wearing long-sleeved shirts and pants instead of T-shirts and shorts, tucking the pant legs into socks, and spraying clothing around entry points – neck, wrists, and ankle areas – as well as exposed flesh. (You might think that hiking in long clothing would be uncomfortable, but it doesn't have to be. Check out mail-order sporting goods outfitters, such as Cabela's and L.L. Bean. They sell clothing made of cool, lightweight material to protect Florida fishermen from the ravages of the sun. The stuff works fine for hikers in the Great Lakes region, also.)

3. *Drink before you feel thirsty*. You will probably carry some kind of rucksack or fanny pack on your hikes, hauling items such as camera, binoculars, notebook, field guides, even lunch. Be sure to add a water bottle, and if you don't carry a bag,

be sure at least to carry a water bottle or canteen. While hiking, most of the time you will not be near potable water.

4. *Be aware of hunters.* The fall of the year is a beautiful time to be afield in Michigan, whether hiking, bird-watching, picnicking, or hunting. Most spots mentioned in this book are located on public lands and many are in areas where hunting is allowed. If you head out between September 15 and January 1, show a sense of safety and respect, both for yourself and the hunters. Wear a cap or vest of fluorescent ("hunter's") orange.

5. *Choose your time wisely.* The best time to spot wildlife is early in the morning and at dusk, especially in the spring of the year. Animals are generally more active in the spring, and the foliage hasn't filled in yet. On a daily basis, they tend to rest during daylight hours and move to their feeding areas in the morning and again before dark. You can also apply this concept to early morning forest road drives and river floats. Only minutes after daybreak I've come across a coyote, a bobcat, and a baker's dozen of elk on slow drives down dirt roads and have seen countless deer and one moose while in the canoe. By the way, deer, elk, and moose present themselves as horizontal masses in a world of vertical trees.

TERMS DEFINED

Major highways are identified in one of three ways:

I – Interstate

US – federal highway

M – state highway

Motor vehicle permit – a required window sticker for entrance to state parks and recreation areas; also a separate sticker required for entrance to Huron-Clinton Metroparks; both daily and seasonal permits are available; a seasonal pass to either state or

Metroparks represents one of the best outdoor bargains you'll find.

DNR—Michigan Department of Natural Resources.

SECTIONS OF THE STATE

Major highways and geography made it easy to divide the state into the five sections covered in this book.

The Lower Peninsula is bisected from south to north by US 127, which becomes US 27, then joins I-75. From west to east, US 10 basically chops the fingers from the palm and thumb of the mitten that is the Lower Peninsula. The Upper Peninsula stands alone.

Section 1 is the Southeast, the portion of the state south of US 10 and east of US 127/27.

Section 2, the Southwest, lies below US 10 and to the west of US 127/27.

Section 3, the Northeast, lies north of US 10 and east of US 27/I-75.

The Northwest section lies to the west of that line and north of US 10.

Section 5 is the Upper Peninsula.

Directions are given under the assumption that you have a map of the state that identifies counties and main highways.

1

Southeast

HIDDEN LAKE GARDENS

Described as a "landscape arboretum," Hidden Lake Gardens offers a wonderful selection of flowers, trees, and shrubs, some growing naturally, others cultivated in special greenhouses. It's a place where you'll instinctively switch off the car radio.

Endowed as a public garden and given to Michigan State University in 1945, the gardens currently encompass over 670 acres of rolling countryside in the beautiful Irish Hills area of southern Michigan. Outdoor plant collections include azaleas, magnolias, and wildflowers. Over 2,500 different species and *cultivars*, or horticulturally derived varieties, of woody plants have been established in the gardens since 1960. In fact, almost the entire southern portion of the six miles of developed roadway within the gardens travels through various tree plantings—hawthorn, mountain ash, oak, crabapple, and others.

Other portions of the road system take you through forests, up and down hills, and through the meadows and experimental plantings. Take note of how well the developed landscaping has been designed to blend with the natural features. Even though you're driving, you'll want to take time at several of the pull-outs, to observe things, from those as delicate as a bee hovering over a primrose to those as grand as the hills, the rocks, and Hidden Lake itself. Overlooking one field-rejuvenation project west of the visitors center is a picnic area.

If you've used the word *conservatory* only while playing Clue, you're in for an eye-opener here. Plant species that thrive in four different climates grow in the Conservatory, which is open during normal hours of operation. The tropical house showcases examples of the lush vegetation you'd expect in the tropics. The arid house contains desert plants. In the temperate house, you'll find house plants common to Michigan. And the Japanese bonsai plants displayed in the lath house are as intriguing as they are intricate.

What's additionally interesting about Hidden Lake Gardens is that welcoming you at the entrance is not a finely sculpted example of horticulture but the massive Founder's Rock. This is an example of a *glacial erratic*, a rock that was swept from its native land by a glacier thousands of years ago and left by the retreating glacier as a reminder of its monumental power and authority. Founder's Rock was not left at Hidden Lake Gardens, but it does highlight another important feature of the landscape, another area of focus. At the visitors center you'll learn some basics about the effect of glaciers in Michigan. In fact, if you don't stop at any other place to learn about them, be sure to take time here.

To begin with, you can learn about various land masses formed by glaciers and then go outside to hike to them or climb on them. Moreover, the visitors center is designed so that you can actually see a feature after reading about it. For example, after reading about *interglobate moraines*, you can look out to see one. After reading a bit more, you'll understand why the Irish

Hills area of Michigan is so—hilly. (Moraines are explained in the section on the Eddy Geology Center that follows.) And after learning about the natural death process of lakes—eutrophication—you can peer from the window at Hidden Lake with its advancing shoreline.

Other displays in the building focus on the geography of plants, the origin of plant life, conifers of the Great Lakes area, and plant adaptation in Michigan. These are the best kind of interpretive displays, the ones that give you solid information without weighing you down by going overboard.

Back outside, you might want to traverse some of the five plus miles of foot trails. Careful though. The trails will take you over territory that's been carved and scooped by glaciers. The hiking isn't difficult, but at times you must be prepared for more than just a pleasant stroll. The trails rise and fall, and erosion has exposed many small rocks that were deposited by glaciers. Wear shoes with sturdy soles.

In winter, visitors take pleasant strolls in the snow or visit the Conservatory.

Except for the winter months, the plants and trees at Hidden Gardens provide some kind of color year-round. If flowers and color matter to you, then consider the following schedule: April through autumn: ornamental shrubs and wildflowers. Mid-April through early May: forsythia, narcissus, and primroses. Early May through mid-June: azaleas, cherries, crabapples, dogwood, rhododendron, and tulips. Early May through early June: lilacs. Mid-June to frost: annuals. Mid-September to early November: autumn color.

How to get there: On a highway map, look in the north central part of Lenawee County for the triangle formed by US 12 on the north, M-52 on the east, and M-50 on the south. Hidden Lake Gardens lies five miles west of M-52 on M-50, about two miles west of the town of Tipton. Approaching from the west, take M-50 east off US 12 about 6.5 miles from their intersection at Cambridge Junction.

General information: Hidden Lake Gardens is open 365 days a year. Hours change according to season, with shorter hours from November through March. A fee is charged for each person entering the grounds. Fees are lower on weekdays than they are on weekends and holidays. Annual passes are available. The gift shop at the visitors center sells brochures and booklets that give more detailed information about the gardens.

For current hours, a color pamphlet, or to make reservations for a guided tour, contact Hidden Lake Gardens, Tipton, MI 49287; 517-431-2060.

GERALD E. EDDY GEOLOGY CENTER
AND WATERLOO RECREATION AREA

Take even fleeting notice of most natural aspects of Michigan and you'll find glaciers playing a role, if not in the spotlight then surely not far upstage. This realization should lead you to the Gerald E. Eddy Geology Center. In addition to offering you a general introduction to the geological features of the state, the center gives you specific information that will make your visit to the Waterloo Recreation Area much more than just a walk in the park.

Visitors are greeted by the "Walkway of Michigan Rocks" that leads to the center's entrance. Named after a late chief of the state's Geological Survey Division and director of the Department of Conservation, the center is inviting but not overwhelming with its exhibits of Michigan rocks, minerals, fossils (including a magnificent example of Michigan's state stone, a Petoskey), crystals, and, of course, glacial information.

Kids will have fun in the oversized sandboxes where they

can "dig for minerals" and examine their finds beneath magnifying glasses. As do many interpretive centers that are managed by the DNR, the Eddy Center features a multi-image slide show presentation.

Also, about half a dozen trails of varying lengths pass near the center, including the Geology Trail. This .75-mile-long interpretive pathway explains the geology of the Waterloo area. Allow half an hour for this walk.

Natural Features of the Waterloo Recreation Area

With just over 20,000 acres patched astride the Washtenaw/ Jackson County line between the major cities of Jackson and Ann Arbor, Waterloo is one of the most heavily used areas in the state. Like many other recreation areas administered by the Parks Division of the DNR, Waterloo offers both modern and rustic camping as well as rustic family cabins and mini-cabins. Thirty-five miles of foot trails are complemented by five miles for bicycles and twelve miles of bridle trails and a horsemen's campground and staging area. Among the foot trails is the Waterloo Trail, which hikers can travel in order to connect to another nearby recreation area. This Waterloo-Pickney Trail totals about forty-five miles. All the trails in Waterloo, though ungroomed, are open to cross-country skiers. The immense variation in the landscape of the area adds to the variety of possibilities for outdoor recreational activities: swimming, fishing, picnicking, hunting, nature and wildlife studies, and backpacking. With that in mind, you may want to plan to spend one or more nights here.

As with most other natural areas, there's a chance to see common wildlife such as white-tailed deer and waterfowl. Also, interestingly enough, for some reason woodchucks are fond of scampering around near the entrance road to the Eddy Center, especially in spring.

The unique aspect of Waterloo, however, is its location, which clearly exhibits the work of glaciers and which makes their effect on the originally flat landscape all the more obvious and observable.

According to Alan Wernette, former state park interpreter for the Waterloo Recreation Area, the advance of glaciers over the land thousands of years ago can be compared to the movement of pancake batter on a hot griddle. These massive mountains of ice would break off chunks from the immense bedrock ridges of the Laurentian or "Canadian" Shield in the north and carry the pieces along during their southward flow.

Some of the rocks, ranging in size from gigantic boulders to pebbles, would grind against one another and, along with soil and other debris, be thus transported. Such movement over hundreds of miles served to smooth and round the edges of these rocks. "Not only in Michigan, but anywhere in the world," says Wernette, geologists consider "smooth and rounded edges on rocks as classic give-aways for glaciation. Basically, except in the American West, where wind or riverbeds will wear down rocks, if you are in a spot in the world that wasn't covered with glaciers, you won't commonly find rounded rocks." Also, if you find a rounded boulder in a high, dry area, you can call it a *glacial erratic* because it was deposited by a glacier in a spot where it doesn't belong.

At some point, the massive pancake batter that was the glaciers reached its southernmost point of progress. Waterloo is located very close to that point in Michigan. Various common formations occur as the result of glaciation, and this part of the state is rife with them. One is the *moraine,* or ridge. Moraines are basically piles of dirt, rock, and other debris left by receding glaciers as they linger more or less, melt, then continue to withdraw, kind of as if the glaciers are humongous conveyor belts and this hesitation in movement allows for an accumulation of debris in one spot. Waterloo is located at the intersection of the

Kalamazoo (running east to west) and the Missaukee (running north to south) moraine systems, the confluence of two glaciers, which accounts for the abundance of ridges in the area.

Two examples of another type of formation, a *kame*, appear in Waterloo. A kame is a small, steep hill that is created when meltwater from a glacier deposits sand and gravel alongside gigantic blocks of ice that have broken from the main glacier. When the ice blocks melt, the hills remain. The kames, Pond Lily Lookout and Sackrider Hill, located near the southern edge of the recreation area, afford spectacular vistas. In fact, on a clear day if you turn your back on the rolling ridges to the north, from Sackrider you can gaze out over the Grass Lake outwash plain, which extends about twenty-five miles until the Irish Hills, another set of moraines, rise on the horizon.

Another nature spot to note is the rare Black Spruce Bog on the north end of the recreation area. Wernette says the best way to describe a bog is "like a donut floating in a bowl of milk." Bogs are like islands, patches of land surrounded by water, but the ground is waterlogged. Their main feature has been described as a "floating mat which eventually obliterates the open water." Bogs themselves are common, and there's one at the end of the three-quarter-mile Bog Trail, which you can reach from the Eddy Center. That bog, however, is dominated by trees commonly found in southern Michigan's comparatively warmer climate: red maple and tamarack.

The Black Spruce Bog, as its name implies, is dominated by black spruce trees, found more in the northern climes of Michigan and Canada. So special is this bog that for a while it was the only place in Michigan that the National Park Service had named a Designated Natural Feature.

But if you want to visit, you'd better hurry. Natural succession is taking place and, according to Wernette, the bog "will start to die out within the next hundred years, or so."

Sackrider and Pond Lily are clearly marked on the map of

the recreation area and are easy to get to from I-94. The acreage containing the Black Spruce Bog is marked, but it isn't identified. You can get there from just about anywhere in the recreation area. The following route will keep you on paved roads.

From I-94, take exit 153 north onto Clear Lake Road. Take Clear Lake about 4.5 miles into the hamlet of Waterloo. There, the road bears to the northwest (left) and its name changes to Munith Road. Stay on the road for three more miles to Parks Road, where the pavement ends. Turn north (right) onto Parks and drive about half a mile to where you'll turn west onto Waterloo-Munith Road. A couple hundred yards down the road on the right, between two chunks of private property, state property signs identify the strip of land on which sits the bog.

How to get there: In Washtenaw County, from I-94, take exit 157 north onto Pierce Road. Stay on Pierce until the pavement ends at a T at Bush Road. Turn west (left) onto Bush. On the left, little more than half a mile from the intersection, you'll find the entrance road to the Eddy Geology Center.

General information: Both the Waterloo Recreation Area and the Eddy Geology Center are open year-round. A motor vehicle permit is required for entry.

For maps and brochures, contact the Waterloo Recreation Area, 16345 McClure Road, Route 1, Chelsea, MI 48118; 313-475-8307.

For more specific information about the Eddy Center or to make group reservations, write to the address above or call 313-475-3170.

PHYLLIS HAEHNLE MEMORIAL SANCTUARY

"Our ability to perceive quality in nature begins, as in art, with the pretty," says Aldo Leopold. "It expands through successive stages of the beautiful to values as yet uncaptured by language.

The quality of cranes lies, I think, in this higher gamut, as yet beyond the reach of words."

Sandhill cranes are the world's oldest birds, the avian species most closely descendant from dinosaurs. In "Marshland Elegy," from the "Sketches Here and There" section of *A Sand*

**A young sandhill crane takes a breather
after the arduous work of hatching**

County Almanac, Leopold speaks of the throaty call of these cranes as "the trumpet in the orchestra of evolution."

To witness upward of 2,000 of these trumpets, an experience surely beyond the reach of words, visit the Phyllis Haehnle Memorial Sanctuary on a midafternoon in October. That's the best time of day, for the birds will be returning from nearby feeding fields to the wetlands of Mud Lake to spend the night. It's the best time of year, for the birds are staging, or assembling, for their southern migration.

Actually, this assembly occurs from September to November, but peaks in October. And very early in the morning, with the first hint of dawn, the cranes make their flights out of the sanctuary.

The Haehnle Sanctuary totals about 900 acres and is administered by the Michigan Audubon Society. It's so close to the Waterloo Recreation Area that some of the state's property adjoins it and the sanctuary is clearly identified on the state's map of the rec area.

Alan Wernette, state park interpreter for the Waterloo Recreation Area, says that, during daylight hours, it's possible to see more cranes by traveling along Seymour Road—"See more," get it? He suggests you search areas north of the sanctuary, to the west of Mt. Hope Road and South of M-106 (North Territorial Road). In fall, look to the farm fields, where the birds will poke around for leftover corn from the harvest. In summer, look for fields that are late planted or low, or those that have been left fallow.

How to get there: In Jackson County, from I-94, take exit 147 north on Race Road for about two miles until it ends at a T at Seymour Road. Turn left onto Seymour and follow it for 1.5 miles until you see the parking area for the sanctuary on the right. A footpath leads to the High Crest Overlook.

General information: You can request a brochure about the

Phyllis Haehnle Memorial Sanctuary from the Michigan Audubon Society, 6011 West St. Joseph, Suite 403, P.O. Box 80527, Lansing, MI 48908-0527; 517-886-9144. The brochure includes a map of the sanctuary only.

For an area map, contact the Waterloo Recreation Area, 16345 McClure Road, Route 1, Chelsea, MI 48118; 313-475-8307.

PORT CRESCENT STATE PARK

A full-service overnight destination as a campground, Port Crescent State Park is also a delightful spot for a day of springtime bird-watching. The state park is the piece of public land closest to the tip of Michigan's Thumb, which explains its appeal to birders. The thumb is a major spring flyway for migratory raptors, with the peak flights coming from late March through early May. These birds don't like crossing too much open water, so the thumb, extending as it does into Saginaw Bay, acts as a funnel for birds heading north. As a result, Port Crescent has become one of the top spots in the thumb for watching the migrations.

Some commonly seen species are buteos such as red-tailed, broad-winged, and red-shouldered hawks; marsh hawks, which are harriers; sharp-shinned hawks, which are accipiters; turkey vultures; bald eagles; osprey; and falcons. The area also sees flights of bluebirds and common loons as well as various kinds of terns. And don't forget to watch for egrets and other shorebirds along the Pinnebog River, which borders the eastern edge of the park's day-use area and parallels the park road on the right once you pass the turnout for the public access.

The day-use area is the newest portion of the state park's 565 acres, which include about three miles of sandy shoreline along Lake Huron. While a 1,000-foot boardwalk transports

A LAKESHORE ECOSYSTEM

If you are planning to visit Port Crescent for a nature tour, you'll also want to stop at the nearby Huron County Nature Center. While it's been in existence for over fifty years, this 120-acre plot has only recently undergone development, and its transformation is not complete.

To get to the Huron County Nature Center, stay on M-25 for about two miles past the entrance to the Port Crescent day-use area. Turn south (left) onto Oak Beach Road. Take that about a quarter mile to Loosemore Road. Turn left and you'll find the parking lot about a quarter mile down on your left.

Birders like the area, for if they are lucky they will be able to observe the kettles—or groups—of hawks heading toward the coast. While the mature hardwoods make for more difficult raptor viewing than at Port Crescent, they also attract dozens of other species, some during migration, others on a year-round basis. Some birds to look for are the crested flycatcher, scarlet tanager, wood thrush, American redstart, and at least ten different species of warblers that migrate through the area.

The jack pines, blueberries, and trailing arbutus—rare for this part of the state—indicate a sandy soil. According to the master plan for the nature center, the "conditions are similar to those found at the turn of the century—one of the few remaining examples of lakeshore ecosystem in Huron County." Of note is the fact that white pines are missing. That's because those that weren't logged out were destroyed in two major fires that consumed the thumb in 1871 and 1881. No more white pines means no more seeds from which white pines can sprout. Though now covered with vegetation, the sandy ridges here, which parallel Lake Huron's shoreline a quarter mile away, indicate that the lake probably extended farther inland than it does today.

This relatively small area is special also because of the diverse ecosystem types that appear here: both dry and moist woods, scrub/shrub wetland, and scrub and wooded lowland. So too do several species of wildflowers: white trillium, pink lady's slipper, and slender blue flag.

Some trails already exist, but planners envisioned a three-mile network of trails covering all those ecosystem types. A planned

nature center building will serve as both a headquarters and an education center.

You can request brochures of the area, including one for a guided hike, by contacting the Huron County Nature Center, Room 211, County Building, 250 East Huron Avenue, Bad Axe, MI 48413.

---

visitors across the small dunes here, the parking area is remarkably flat, almost low. The reason for this is simple. The sand here is so fine that it was mined and shipped out for glassmaking. The parking area represents the spot where much of the sand was scraped away.

What makes Port Crescent delightful as a birding spot is that while here you can do more than just scan the skies for birds. The beach, picnic areas, and nearby woods offer other possibilities.

The camping area is located across the river where the town of Port Crescent once stood. From the day-use area you can see a chimney that rises above the modern campground, a solitary reminder of the former settlement.

Between the day-use area and that campground, on an island formed by the Pinnebog and an old river channel, lie a rustic campground reserved for the use of youth organizations and a 2.5-mile foot trail that doubles as a cross-country ski trail.

How to get there: In Huron County, take M-53 (Van Dyke Road) north from the town of Bad Axe for about fourteen miles to Port Crescent Road. Take Port Crescent west for about two miles until it dead-ends at M-25 (Port Austin Road). Turn left onto M-25 and drive 1.1 miles to the entrance of the park's day-use area.

General information: The park is open year-round. A motor vehicle permit is required for entry. For maps, brochures, and the seasonal hours for the day-use area, contact Port Crescent State Park Manager, 6573 State Park Road, Caseville, MI 48725; 517-738-8663.

If you are planning an extended stay in the area, you might also contact the Greater Port Austin Area Chamber of Commerce, P.O. Box 274, Port Austin, MI 48467; 517-738-7600.

ST. CLAIR FLATS STATE WILDLIFE AREA

This is the one spot I knew I wanted to include in this book from the get-go. As the area where the St. Clair River spreads out before emptying into Lake St. Clair, the Flats represent the largest freshwater delta in the country. Historically, they've been as important to this area as has the Mississippi River in its many incarnations to towns from St. Louis to Memphis to New Orleans. While the St. Clair River itself is an important link in the water route connecting the Great Lakes, the Flats have traditionally teemed with wildlife and have, for that reason, attracted the attention of humans. If you share my taste for nature and history, you'll be glad you scheduled a trip to this part of Michigan.

St. John's Marsh is an ideal spot for a springtime flat-water paddle if you have a canoe. Ducks, geese, other waterfowl, swans, egrets, herons, and wetland songbirds such as red-winged blackbirds abound.

Don't expect massive areas of open, big water. A shallow, narrow canal leads north from the access to more open areas of the marsh. Another canal follows the road back west, then north. In fact, fishermen usually stand post along Dyke Road at the edge of the canal there.

If you float later in the summer, the water may be too shallow in some spots for your canoe to glide over easily. Also, the reeds and bulrushes will have grown higher and higher, creating little pockets of water that you may wander around in and even

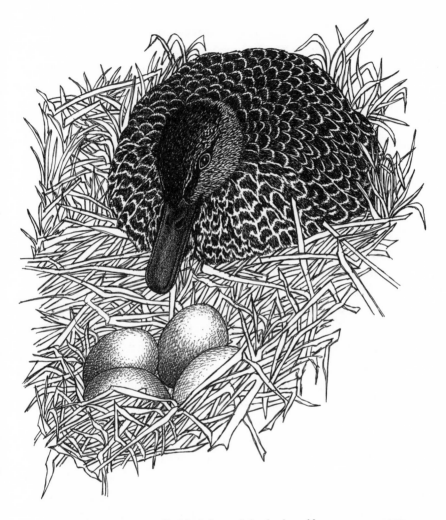

Black ducks are not really black but subtle shades of brown, gray, green, and blue with iridescent purple wing patches and silver underwings

get turned around. Not to worry, for eventually you'll have to return to the main body of water and then to one of the canals. Dyke Road is a very busy thoroughfare, and its traffic, which you soon learn to tune out as you paddle, can also act as a beacon if you find yourself too far in the tall reeds to see your way clear.

One Mother's Day, I topped our Cherokee with my solo canoe and headed out to St. John's Marsh. After about two hours of wandering and watching, of paddling and listening, I felt revived, satisfied. That's the best way to approach a visit to St. John's Marsh. It's easy to get to but not so large that it will attract lots of people and motorboats. Moreover, the pleasant paddling and the wildlife viewing opportunities represent a little respite from the real world, which remains as close as the traffic on Dyke Road.

If you visit St. John's Marsh in spring, you may as well allow yourself time to head over to Harsens Island.

A traditional hunting ground, site of salt mines, and burial place for local as well as roving Indians, Harsens Island is really a collection of small islands joined by dozens of small bridges over various-sized canals. In fact, when, around the turn of the century, the Flats area became known as "the Venice of America," Harsens Island was almost as popular a summer vacation spot as Newport or Atlantic City in the East. So popular was Harsens that it remains the only island in the state containing the entire length of a state trunkline, M-154.

Tradition holds that the first white men to gaze upon the jewel that is Harsens Island were the explorers La Salle and Father Hennepin. History shows that the island was leased to Jacob Harson and two partners in 1697, when some land deeds in Detroit were still recorded in French. It was also a time when the Indians—but not the whites—had to attest in the lease that they were sober at the time of signing.

Legend holds that a term of the lease has become the source of a piece of modern slang. Harson and his partners agreed to pay the Chippewa (Ojibwa) an annual sum of "one hundred dollars, or bucks, or value thereof, in clothing and other necessaries," for a period of six years. Locals believe this is the earliest use of the term *buck* for "one dollar."

Harsens Island has also remained popular for another reason, waterfowl hunting. It has been rated in importance alongside the Saginaw and Chesapeake Bays by waterfowl enthusiasts. If you take the road to the headquarters of the St. Clair Flats State Wildlife Area, especially in spring, you should easily be able to see why.

A series of dikes, canals, water gates, and cornfields makes this spot paradise for waterfowl. And don't underestimate their intelligence. On more than one occasion during duck season, I paddled out after shooting hours had ended, having seen only three or four high-flying ducks all day. But signaled by the retreating sun as it radiated purple around the clouds, thousands of ducks—almost as thick as in Alfred Hitchcock's *The Birds*—flooded into the floodings.

In spring, however, the birds aren't pressured away by hunters, so they'll be more visible and more at ease. And the corn isn't high yet. In fact, one Good Friday afternoon, I sat in the parking lot at the headquarters and watched fifteen white-tailed deer run across the field to the southwest, a sight impossible to behold once the crops start to flourish in summer. Also, the area directly behind the headquarters is a preserve, so you can usually see birds there, spring through fall. Or you can drive along any of the roads, especially at the southwest end of the island, find a parking spot, and watch the ducks flying. Sometimes, you can see small flocks no matter in which direction you look. Mallards and black ducks are the most visible species.

Take M-154 where it become Bates Drive below Clays Landing, along the leg that extends from the southwest end of the island. On the right is Little Muscamoot Bay, and you should be able to see some open-water species of ducks such as redheads, scaup, American goldeneyes, and though rare, canvasbacks. A view of these ducks *rafting*, or floating in a concentration, will show you why waterfowlers pattern their decoy spreads so precisely.

How to get there:

Canoeists: From I-94 in Macomb County, take exit 243 onto M-29 east toward New Baltimore in St. Clair County. For about six miles outside New Baltimore, M-29 curves around Anchor Bay of Lake St. Clair. It then changes to a straightaway (Dyke Road), heading almost due south for little more than two miles, with the bay on the right and St. John's Marsh on the left. You'll see what appears to be a lighthouse in the distance. This marks the "Colony" subdivision. Stay on the road as it curves past the "Colony." Ahead on the left about a quarter mile, you'll see a state-maintained public access to the marsh.

Car tour: Stay on M-29 as it passes the public access. About two miles later, you'll see signs for the car ferry to Harsens Island. Once you land on the island, take M-154 to the left. A little more than a mile down the road, just past the school on the left, you'll cross a bridge and the road will begin to curve left. Slow down for that curve and turn right onto the dirt road that enters the highway. Follow that road to the left, then straight down to the headquarters of the St. Clair Flats State Wildlife Area.

General information: The ferry to Harsens Island is run by a private company. The fare will be collected as you cross. Lots of people still consider Harsens Island a vacation destination, and lots of islanders commute to work in the city. So you can expect longer lines to get on the ferry during rush hours and on weekends. The crossing takes only about five minutes, however, and the ferries run quite regularly during peak seasons.

You can pick up a map of the St. Clair Flats State Wildlife Area at the headquarters, but you want to call first. Budget constraints on the DNR have restricted the hours during which technicians are available. Try calling 810-748-9504 mornings, after 8:30 and before noon.

HURON-CLINTON METROPARKS

Imagine a crescent beginning near the mouth of the Clinton River at Lake St. Clair near the base of Michigan's Thumb, extending inland to just past Ann Arbor, then running back southeastward following the Huron River to its mouth at Lake Erie. Sprinkle that crescent with several parks preserved for public recreation and appreciation of natural resources. This image best describes the layout of the Huron-Clinton Metroparks, and it best describes the initial vision for the Metroparks dating from the late 1930s. About the only item missing from the original plan is a single road to connect all the parks. While that road didn't materialize, its memory remains, for in Macomb County, 16 Mile Road bears the name Metropolitan Parkway for the last several miles of its length before it ends at Metro Beach Metropark.

To get a precise idea of what these parks represent, just dissect their collective name. They take advantage of the natural beauty and resources provided by the two major rivers in southeastern Michigan, the Huron and the Clinton. They are parks, carefully cultivated and developed to attract human visitors. And they are located in the metropolitan Detroit area. In fact, over 60 percent of Michigan's population lives within a half hour's drive of one or more of the parks. So if you visit a Metropark, don't expect a wilderness experience enhanced by solitude.

To begin with, several of the parks have swimming beaches or pools and all but one have picnic areas. As a result, they are popular for family and group outings. Almost half of them have golf courses. Four parks — Metro, Stony Creek, Kensington, and Lake Erie — are located on lakes or impoundments large enough to accommodate motorboats and have boat launches. The two on Michigan's east coast — Metro and Lake Erie — also have marinas. Realize that these parks were designed with the philosophy of encouraging city folk to get outdoors, and you'll understand why they offer such amenities.

But can an outdoor purist find some quiet time and space in a Metropark? Yep. Is it possible to get away from the crowd? Certainly. Are some of the areas big enough and wild enough that you can get lost if you aren't careful? Absolutely. You do yourself a disservice if you dismiss these parks based merely on the fact that they draw lots of visitors. If that matters to you, then try adopting the strategy that has helped me out: if you get there early in the day, you can begin the return trip of your hike or ski or bike ride before the others hit the trails. If you keep quiet, you may be joined by some nonhuman companions.

This strategy paid off one winter morning, for example, when my wife and I had followed the snowplow into the parking lot at Stony Creek. Consequently, we were the first to hit the cross-country ski trail. About an hour later, we were skiing back toward the parking area when two beautiful white-tailed deer, still in full antlers, came bounding down the trail toward us. We simply waited for them to notice us and skip off the trail. Once their commotion faded, we could easily hear from up the trail the human voices that had spooked them our way. So, at the very least, the Metroparks offer some unencumbered areas where nature lovers can roam around and where they stand a chance to see wildlife common to the state.

The other reason to give the Metroparks the nod is the fact that most of them have dedicated nature study areas.

You may be surprised at what awaits at the Metroparks. For an idea, let's tour that crescent I asked you to imagine earlier, stopping at each park along the way.

Metro Beach (Macomb County)

Birders will be pleased to know that Metro Beach is one of the top bird-watching areas in the state. The park's location and variety of habitat combine to entice large numbers of birds throughout the year. The park is located on a point that juts into Lake St. Clair and, as a result, attracts migrating birds. Leslie Sutton, the supervising naturalist at the park, describes this attraction to be "like freeway rest stops are for people." Since all birds follow the same general migration routes, visitors can expect to see sandpipers and shorebirds, robins, songbirds, and warblers in addition to waterfowl, she says, and mentions three primary areas for bird-watching in the park.

The first is the North Marsh, where, depending on how much water is present, you can find sandpipers, shorebirds, and some shallow-water puddle ducks like wood ducks, mallards, and shovelers. That area is also great for blue herons and dunlins.

The North Marsh is located along the park's exit route. You have to park in the boat launch area and walk to it. No marked trail exists, just park property that's mowed.

If any open water remains during winter months, look for hundreds of ducks and geese to remain behind while their cousins head south. The birds are used to being fed, and while they aren't tame, they are approachable to a degree. Look for them to flock up along the canal side of the North Marina boat launch area.

The second area for birding is the nature trail that runs along the South Marsh, where you'll see most of the warblers, along with herons and marsh wrens.

The third major birding area is along the lake itself at Huron Point, where you'll see the deeper-water diving ducks such as canvasbacks, redheads, and mergansers. The most common gulls here are the ring-billed. During migration, you can identify many that are less common. Just walk to the end of the point and be patient.

Other birds, such as tree sparrows, juncos, and evening grosbeaks, normally live farther north and mark the Metropark as the southern limit of their migrations.

One rare bird that's been sighted is the shrike, which, says

Sutton, is "nicknamed the 'butcher bird.' They're the bird that supposedly picks up a mouse and impales it on a thorn.

"There are also great horned owls nesting in the nature area," she adds.

The nature center includes displays on animals and birds common to the area, a profile of the Lake St. Clair area of the Great Lakes region, and an exhibit highlighting the historical use of the area by the French voyageurs. This exhibit might prove to be additionally interesting, for guided trips aboard the *Voyageur* canoe are scheduled throughout the summer.

Two short hiking trails, three-quarters and one-half mile each, wend through the small woods and along the edge of the South Marsh in the nature study area. Other "natural" activities available at Metro Beach are canoeing, hiking or biking along a paved trail throughout the park, and ice skating. Cross-country ski rentals are handled at the nature center.

Wolcott Mill (Macomb County)

As its name implies, this park's main attraction is a restored gristmill along the North Branch of the Clinton River. The emphasis here is on historical rather than natural interpretation. The park is closed in winter.

Stony Creek (Macomb/Oakland Counties)

The lake here is one of two impounds in the Metroparks. In this case, Stony Creek, a tributary of the Clinton River, was dammed to form a 600-acre lake. Actually, three separate ponds were created by the dams.

Most fishing and boating are done on the main pond, the southernmost. The two beaches are also located here. The bad news is that the canoe rental concession, one of only two in the Metropark system, is also located here. So if you plan to canoe in a rented craft at Stony Creek, you'll probably restrict your travels to the coves at the west end of the lake, well within earshot of the picnickers and boaters.

The good news is that, of the several Metropark nature centers, Stony Creek's is the only one that isn't reached via the main park road. The nature study area is situated more than two miles from the bulk of the action on the southern pond. In fact, the north pond, which is part of the nature study area, is closed to all human interference—canoeing, boating, even shore fishing. As a result, if you seek a quiet spot for relaxation and reflection, the nature center area should provide it.

The center itself is a welcoming building, an old wooden house with a beautiful overlook of the area where the actual creek called "Stony" flows by on its way to the impoundment. The enclosed porch offers a good vantage from which to view the bird feeders and the customers they attract. The various displays present an introduction to animals, insects, and some birds in the area.

The self-guided nature trails wander through some interesting territory: near wetlands, over hills, and through some woodlands. The Reflection Trail covers one-half mile and passes along pond and stream habitats. For one and a quarter miles, the Landscape Trail heads up, over, and down some carvings left behind by the glaciers. The longest, the Habitat Trail winds for 2.5 miles through various habitats, including fields, woods, and wetlands. These are hiking trails only, although a separate cross-country ski trail is maintained near the nature center.

While the nature center is conveniently nestled away from most other activities, that's not to say that you should avoid Stony Creek proper. By no means. A six-mile, paved bike-hike trail follows the main park road and circles the south pond. In the winter, an ice rink is cleared in the boat launch area just south of

Eastwood Beach. Cross-country ski rental is available at the golf course headquarters. Across the park road, near Eastwood, beginners will find agreeable ski trails. Experienced skiers will want to head for the collection of trails and loops near the West Branch sledding area. These include sections rated as "Most Difficult."

The park office is located on a hill that itself is the edge of what was once a glacial lake. From that vantage, you can see the Detroit skyline to the south. It is also the best local spot from which to view Halley's comet. So if you're in the area next time the comet passes through . . .

Indian Springs (Oakland County)

A glance at the map will show you that about two-thirds of this park's 2,232 acres is dedicated as a nature study area. Perhaps that's appropriate, for unlike spots such as Stony Creek and Kensington where the land was developed into parks, Indian Springs was established to preserve a chunk of the Great Huron Swamp from development. Two main branches of the Huron River, its headwaters actually, flow from the swamp, so don't expect any grand area for water sports here.

As at the other nature centers, displays at Indian Springs highlight animals and plants that you're likely to see in the area. Some live snakes as well as some rubber mounts comprise the reptile exhibit. There are also interpretive stations on mushrooms, pond life, and man's relationship with energy – from fire to solar. A "please touch" table invites the kiddies to get their hands on some pelts and antlers.

Three hiking trails are for self-guided tours. The Woodland Trail is a 3.5-mile loop that cuts through the swampland woods of the area. Three shortcuts offer choices for a shorter hike, while the Timberland Lake Walk is a one-eighth-mile spur that takes the hiker back to a small lake. According to Steve Horn, supervising naturalist at Indian Springs, this is a "unique little habitat." Along this spur,which traverses a bog edge, you'll be able to see several species of orchids and pitcher plants. The tamarack and poison sumac give a "northern Michigan feel" to this spot. Another spur, back near the nature center, takes hikers up a small hill and gives them a view of the fields and forests in the area as well as the bike path and golf course.

Farmland Trail heads through old fields and takes a loop into the woods on its 1.5-mile tour. And at one-third mile, the hard-surfaced Pondside Trail is the easiest of the three to negotiate. It offers a good view of pond life.

Horn says that it's possible to glimpse deer, foxes, and raccoons, although the animals here seem "wilder" than at the other parks. So if you want to see them, you have to get out there when the animals are active: early morning and just before dark. Some special bird species here include pileated woodpeckers and barred owls.

There's also an eight-mile hike-bike trail-with-loop, part of which is not paved; a picnic area; and a "tot lot" play area.

Cross-country ski rental is available at the golf course shack. Ski paths are set on the bike-hike trail, the golf course, and along the Farmland Trail. Skiing is allowed on the other trails, though school children on field trips usually chew up the snow nearest to the nature center.

Kensington (Oakland/Livingston Counties)

If Steve Horn says the wildlife is "wilder" at Indian Springs than at other areas, perhaps he had Kensington's nature study area in mind. For there, according to naturalist Lynn Kavanagh, it's "easy to see deer, real easy."

Four trails of varying length emanate from the nature center at Kensington. They cover a variety of territory, including fields, forests and hills, but especially a lot of wetlands: marsh and swamp. These trails are the Tamarack (0.5 mile), Deer Run (1.5 to 1.75 miles), Aspen (1.3 miles), and Wildwing (2.5 miles). The Chickadee loop off Deer Run isn't as well traveled as the others. Neither is the Fox Trail, which leads from Deer Run through some fields and connects to Chickadee.

Some other wildlife species you may see include a variety of squirrels, birds—both migratory and year-round species like chickadees, tufted titmice, and various woodpeckers—snakes, turtles, and muskrats. Other species that are present but which you aren't likely to see are mink, raccoon, and both gray and red fox.

Displays in the nature center change with the season. You may find, for example, information on bluebirds, the solar system, or park animals and what they eat.

The trails in the nature study area are for foot travel only. Although cross-country skis are rented from the golf starter shack, skiing is allowed only on the golf course, the 8.25-mile bike-hike loop that follows the park road and encircles Kent Lake, and the little spurs that shoot from that trail toward the interior of the park.

As one of the impounds among the Metroparks' waters, Kensington is a popular spot for families and groups that are looking for a day on some bigger water. Although there is no canoe rental, visitors with their own canoes may want to paddle around amid the islands. Notice that Labadie Island can be reached only by boat.

Huron Meadows (Livingston County)

About a mile and a half of the Huron River nearly bisects this park, but the real attraction is the tiny Maltby Lake. No private boats are allowed on the lake; boats may be rented at the golf shack. A short hike along a trail gets you to the docks where the boats are kept.

Maltby is a ten- to fifteen-acre spring-fed lake that gets about forty feet deep. It provides a quiet, relaxing spot not too far from the crowd if you just want to row around.

A cross-country ski rental is also housed in the golf shack.

Hudson Mills, Dexter-Huron, Delhi (Washtenaw County)

These three parks are grouped together because their boundaries nearly touch. In fact, they are connected by water, but some private property is mixed in, so park officials urge patrons to be considerate. From Hudson Mills to Delhi is about ten miles by car, eight by river.

As with virtually all other Metroparks, these three are carefully sculpted to make them appealing as day-use areas for people in the nearby cities, with picnic areas, shelters, and ball fields. At Hudson Mills, one leg of the mostly wooded Acorn Nature Trail runs along the Huron River's bank. There's also a bike-hike path. Bikes and cross-country skis may be rented at the park office. Although there's no nature center here, interpretive programs are held year-round.

Hudson Mills has a canoe campground for people planning to arrive by canoe and leave by canoe. You need to notify the park office beforehand of your intentions to stay. Other than that, there are no launch sites at any of these three parks, and they may not be used after closing. Day-trippers can rent canoes at Delhi or hire the concessionaire to shuttle them and their own canoes upriver to Hudson Mills.

Lower Huron, Willow, Oakwoods (Wayne County)

Like the previous group, these parks are linked because they are connected, both by water and by narrow strips of land.

Strung along the river like Christmas popcorn on a string,

these are the parks to visit if you want to take a lengthy canoe ride down the river as it twists and turns for about twelve miles before flowing into the spreads of bayous, marshes, and oxbows that become the "Walk-in-the-Water" self-guided canoe trail on the backwaters of the Flat Rock impoundment. Or near the Oakwoods nature center, you can launch right in the middle of the water trail. But you have to bring your own canoe—no rentals in these parks. At the Oakwoods nature center or Lower Huron's park office you can pick up a map that indicates both times and distances for a float through the three parks.

At Lower Huron, the Bob White and Paw Paw Nature Trails, short little loops, offer the chance for self-guided hikes. You can pick up a brochure explaining points of interest at the park office.

Separate bike-hike trails run the length of Lower Huron (about four miles) and around the bulk of Willow (4.5 miles). Both parks sport swimming pools and ice skating rinks. Willow also has a cross-country ski rental at the pool-activity area.

Of the three parks here, Oakwoods is the only one with a nature study area, 400 acres set aside near the Huron River.

In addition to the water trail, four other trails of varying length loop away from this center. Splitlog is a hard-surface, all-weather trail particularly inviting to special needs visitors: handicapped, elderly, and parents with baby strollers. It leads to a river overlook. Self-guided cassette tapes for this 700-foot trail are available at the nature center. Big Tree circles for three-quarters of a mile through a stand of hardwoods and crosses an ancient glacial sandbar. Sky-Come Down, a mile long, traverses some woods, some fields, and some edges as it curves past a small pond. The Long Bark trail, two miles, heads out along the Huron River and then dips into the deep woods for the return trip to the park road. Interpretive leaflets for each of these trails are available in the nature center.

According to Glen Dent, naturalist at Oakwoods, about 175

species of birds have been identified at Oakwoods, including bald eagles and osprey.

The nature center at Oakwoods has displays of cold-blooded animals like snakes and turtles native to the area, an aquarium of fish from the river, and mounts of other animals native to Michigan. An observation room overlooks both the river and some bird feeders that attract ducks and geese as well as songbirds.

Finally, a horse staging area and five miles of horse trails are available at Oakwoods from April through October for riders obtaining an advanced release from the park office.

Lake Erie (Wayne County)

Completing the crescent, the nearly 1,600 acres of this Metropark have been molded almost entirely for the benefit of people who don't want to leave too much of the city behind them. A wave pool, golf course, and marina are some of the highlights. Cross-country ski rental is available at the pool area, where ice skating also takes place.

The real draw of this Metropark is the new Lake Erie Marshlands Museum and Nature Center, scheduled for a spring 1995 opening. According to Paul Cypher, provisional interpreter at Lake Erie, "Since we're located on a marsh, the entire aspect of the nature center is marshlands." Two wings of the building will separate the natural history from the cultural history of the area. Gerald Wykes, curator/supervising interpreter, says that the museum, at 7,100 square feet, is the largest facility the Huron-Clinton Metropark Authority has opened to the public and represents the culmination of twenty years of planning.

In the nature wing, a 1,300-gallon-capacity aquarium will feature open-water Great Lakes species such as walleye and perch. Three smaller aquaria will profile the three types of water environments of the park: marsh, bay, and open water. This second open-water exhibit will display alien species of fish, plants, and other creatures like the zebra mussel. As a teaching facility, the museum will feature seasonal exhibits and displays of plant and wildlife ecology and coastal environments.

Much of the unique cultural history of this "Downriver" area of Michigan is centered around a lifestyle dependent on the land and the resources offered here and the traditional methods of taking advantage of them. For example, expect to find exhibits explaining ice harvesting, commercial fishing, and trapping.

The focal point, says Wykes, is the museum's emphasis on waterfowl hunting. Exhibits will include mounted specimens, decoy carving, hunting dogs—anything associated with waterfowl hunting from the times when people hunted for the market through the "golden age" of waterfowling (1870s to 1940s) to the present.

Currently, a five-mile trail system is planned with several loops beginning at the museum. Wykes says the trail planners are trying to integrate the four different coastal environments that exist in the park: lowland thicket, upland woods, open fields, and the coastal marsh itself. While walking along the marsh, be alert for shorebirds such as great blue herons and egrets. Mad splashing in the shallows during spring may indicate spawning carp.

How to get there: The thirteen current Huron-Clinton Metroparks are situated throughout five counties in southeastern Michigan. The simplest way to locate each of them is to consult the free map you can order from the Huron-Clinton Metropark Authority (HCMA).

General information: A motor vehicle permit is required for entrance to all Metroparks. Note that this is *not* the same as the permit to get into state parks. You can purchase either daily or seasonal passes.

Except for Wolcott Mill, closed in winter, the parks and

their nature centers are open year-round, with seasonally adjusted hours. Best to check beforehand, for the nature centers' hours of operation are usually more restricted than those of the parks in general.

Another reason to check beforehand is that, throughout the year, special interpretive programs are held at the various nature centers, some even in the dark of night. For these, plus for the *Voyageur* canoe rides, reservations are required. Also, horse riders should be sure to contact Oakwoods before coming to the park.

Be sure to request the current "Metropark Guide" from the HCMA. This guide to the Metroparks is also the best five-county road map available. Plus it's free. You can also request pamphlets that detail the Metroparks of your choice. Write the HCMA at 13000 High Ridge Drive, P.O. Box 2001, Brighton, MI 48116-8001.

Or you can phone 800-47-PARKS (477-2757). The best thing about this number is that the operator here can connect you to any park or nature center that you desire.

WEST BLOOMFIELD WOODS NATURE PRESERVE

It's hard to believe that in the middle of the most affluent county in the state, within shouting distance of a subdivision, there sits a 162-acre parcel of land that has been designated as an Urban Wildlife Sanctuary. Such is the case, however, of the West Bloomfield Woods Nature Preserve, which was accorded this national distinction in 1992, the first so named in the state.

If you find yourself stuck in southeastern Michigan or in Detroit's northern suburbs on business or in town for a wedding or something and you feel the need for a booster shot of rejuvenation from nature, head to West Bloomfield Woods.

A couple of foot trail loops traverse the preserve proper.

And make no mistake. These are footpaths only; no bicycles or horses are allowed. The first loop, half a mile long, is eight feet wide and is designed for the ease of handicappers. The other trail, 2.1 miles long, is five feet wide and covered with wood chips. Additionally, the West Bloomfield Trail Network Greenway, a leg of the "Rails to Trails system," extends 4.25 miles between the parking area and Sylvan Manor Park to the east. This trail is open to hikers, cross-country skiers, and bicyclists.

Visitors to the preserve may be surprised at the myriad species of plants and animals that abound here. Over 100 species of birds have been observed here, from owls and hawks to red-winged blackbirds and several types of woodpeckers. Observant visitors will also see signs of white-tailed deer, mink, even red fox. The wetlands play host to ducks and muskrats, various frogs and turtles, and the locally endangered blue-spotted salamander. Probably the feature with the greatest appeal is the great blue heron rookery on the eastern side of the preserve.

Plant lovers will find more than 100 species of wildflowers and abundant tree and shrub life. In the spring, white trilliums and yellow trout lilies line the forest floor beneath the oak, hickory, aspen, and elm trees. Other common flowers are the columbine, white baneberry, and yellow iris. Some of the other trees and shrubs to look for are hawthorn, chokecherry, Juneberry, dogwood, and honeysuckle.

For a relatively small parcel of land, the preserve contains remarkably diverse ecosystem types. For example, its boundaries enclose all or parts of no fewer than eight wetlands of various sizes, plus a creek. There are clumps of hardwoods, hills that include a glacial moraine, and swamps. In fact, the short loop has a boardwalk that extends over a small wetland. This is a nice place to call "time out" and to try to imagine all the organisms that depend on healthy wetlands and to realize that the health of a wetland is not indicated by crystal clear waters devoid of weeds.

How to get there: In Oakland County, from I-696, take the Orchard Lake Road exit north. Follow Orchard Lake for five miles to the Y at Pontiac Trail. Take Pontiac Trail (left branch of the Y) for 1.5 miles to Arrowhead. Turn south onto Arrowhead and continue for a quarter mile to the parking area.

General information: Parking and admission to the preserve are free. It is open daily from 8:00 A.M. to sunset. If you visit the preserve on a warm summer night, be sure to apply a liberal dose of insect repellent.

Info boxes at the parking area/trailhead are meant to contain interpretive brochures/maps, but they are popular items. To be sure you have a brochure for the preserve and for the trail network, contact West Bloomfield Parks and Recreation, 3325 Middlebelt Road, West Bloomfield, MI 48323; 810-334-5660.

SHIAWASSEE NATIONAL WILDLIFE REFUGE

U.S. Fish and Wildlife people refer to this area as an "oasis of wetland and woodland for migratory birds and resident wildlife," and it's easy to understand why. This 9,000-acre parcel rests at the confluence of five rivers: the Flint, Cass, Bad, Tittabawassee, and Shiawassee. Together with several other creeks they combine to form the river that flows through the nearby town and into the bay, all three of which share the same name: Saginaw. All this water is a major attractant for birds along the Mississippi Flyway, and the Shiawassee National Wildlife Refuge has been called one of the top bird-viewing areas in the country. The block of land that constitutes the refuge is otherwise surrounded by land that has been developed. In other words, as the available habitat in this naturally appealing area has shrunk, the refuge, with its expanses of undisturbed and minimally disturbed land, has become more valuable to animals and migratory birds. As a result, over 190 species of birds are commonly attracted to this place.

And that explains why humans come here, too. The Fish and Wildlife Service maintains two pathways that are open year-round from dawn to dusk. Visitors are encouraged to hike, bike, or cross-country ski on the trails. Also, Shiawassee is one of only two national refuges in the state that are staffed and have head-quarters where your questions can be answered.

The southern trail, a five-mile loop, provides probably the better view and better chance to see wildlife. At the farthest out-bound point of the trail stands an observation tower from which vantage you can easily tell why the historic name for this area is the Flats. With so many rivers, much of the area consists of bot-tomland hardwoods, grasses, and shallow marshes. Much of the area is diked to keep water in—or out—as needed. Coupled with the agricultural fields that are carefully managed to provide food for the birds that stop by during their southern migration in the fall, the natural landscape seems so flat you might mistake it for the Great Plains.

Surprisingly, the hardwoods play an important role here. If this weren't a refuge, the trees would be considered an obstruc-tion and would be cut down. Their stumps would be removed, and more of the nutrition-rich soil would be converted to agricul-tural use. But they are left to stand, and seasonal flooding in the area has produced a "green tree reservoir," and in the fall the nuts from these hardwoods—green ash, red and silver maples, and white oak—drop into the water and become food for the water-fowl. For example, believe it or not, wood ducks will thrive on acorns when they can find them.

This southern trail might be a good choice for a quick bike trip in the spring if you want to observe things from the tower but don't want to hike the entire loop.

The northern trail is a bit shorter, a little more than a four-mile loop, and goes through woods. Since this area is more sheltered from the sun and wind than the other trail, the snow tends to last a little longer. This is the trail of choice for most cross-country skiers.

Because of the primarily flat terrain, both loops offer very easy hiking, skiing, or biking. About the biggest inconveniences you may face are bugs in summer or flooded trails during times of high water.

The greatest opportunity to see loads of migratory birds is at the peaks of migration, March through April and September through November. During these times don't be surprised to see thousands and thousands of waterfowl. Probably the easiest animal to view, however, is the white-tailed deer, which can be seen just about all year long.

How to get there: In Saginaw County, south of Saginaw, from M-13 turn west onto Curtis Road. Continue on Curtis for three-quarters of a mile to the refuge headquarters, where you can pick up a map to the open trails.

General information: If you are planning a visit to see certain species of birds, the Fish and Wildlife people recommend you call to get up-to-date information on the migration and any weather conditions that might be affecting the birds.

For pamphlets on the area or maps, write or call: Refuge Manager, Shiawassee National Wildlife Refuge, 6975 Mower Road, RR 1, Saginaw, MI 48601; 517-777-5930.

Be sure to request the "Birds of Shiawassee National Wildlife Refuge" pamphlet. It contains a list of all the species common to the refuge plus the normal seasons for viewing them and their relative abundance.

CHIPPEWA NATURE CENTER

It's risky to imagine that such a wonderful nature center can thrive so close to a moderately big city, Midland, and in the shadow of one of the nation's largest producers of unnatural products, Dow Chemical. But there it is, at the confluence of the Pine and Chippewa Rivers, the 900-acre Chippewa Nature Center, a privately funded project that's open to the public.

After following the signs, you'll arrive at what appears to be an elementary school, though it's actually the visitors center. The look is appropriate, however, for the people at the center have done their work, and if you do yours, some education will take place during your visit.

A small but thorough museum offers a peek at the geology, archaeology, and nature of the Saginaw Valley. You'll get a refresher course in glacial action on the land, but there's much more. Displays explain the various strata of rock and sediment that now lie thousands of feet below ground but which, millions of years ago, made up the earth's surface. During your stroll through the museum, I defy you to gaze at the life-size model of the giant beaver without uttering a "Wow!" when the reality of its size finally strikes you.

Among the displays and dioramas depicting both ancient and modern Indian life in the Saginaw Valley two modern samples of Indian work, really Indian art, stand out. Marvel at the craftsmanship behind production of the handmade birch-bark canoe, and take time to study the stylized carvings of birds, waterfowl, snakes, and ducks by "Smokey" Joe Jackson.

You'll see these carvings on your way to the wildlife feeding station. Don't let the term mislead you. This is not a spot at which you feed the animals. Rather, it's a spot, still inside the comfort of the building, from which you can view the birds and animals that come to feed. An outdoor microphone captures the sounds of the feeding yard, which emanate from a speaker inside and add a pleasing and calm tone to the viewing area. Visit near the beginning of any month, and you may be the one to record the first appearance, that month, for any number of species. If you're lucky, you may be on hand when the white-tailed deer or wild turkeys sneak in for some chow.

The visitors center also has a touch table, where children are invited to handle the merchandise, and a river overlook from where, even during the most disagreeable weather, you can surrender yourself to the serenity of the impassive river as it flows along on its daily routine.

Adding to the center's school-like character are a library and classrooms. These are important to note, for if you find yourself staying in the Midland area for a few days, you may want to attend one of the several interpretive workshops the center sponsors throughout the year. Various programs are geared for adults and children and are held both indoors and out.

Outside, about a dozen different trails await you, offering loops from 0.3 to 3.1 miles in length. Just as variable are the degrees of development of the trails, from paths worn on the grass, to wood chips, to paved and handicapped accessible.

From these trails, you may see the deer and turkeys, an occasional red fox, some minks along the riverbanks, as well as beavers, which, according to the management policy of the center, are being left to do whatever work they may do. Beaver work, plus the fact that the center is located in a floodplain, sometimes means that parts of the trails are sloppy or downright impassible.

You can get in good birding year-round here, not spectacular, but consistent. Wood ducks often breed here, and Canada geese and great blue herons are common. Northern-breeding birds, such as goldeneyes, buffleheads, and various mergansers, sometimes stop in for brief visits. The combination of wet wooded areas alongside or near several open fields also makes this a good spot to watch the woodcock mating dance in spring. In the newly opened Wetlands area, common and black terns have been spotted.

THE DANCE OF THE WOODCOCK

Unless you're a serious birder or a hunter, you probably have no idea what a woodcock looks like or what is meant by its mating dance. But you don't have to be a serious birder in order to observe one of these moonlit flights of fancy. In fact, it is arguably the most predictable, easiest to see, yet most uncommonly viewed animal behavior available to you in the state. And even if you don't partake of this delicious game bird in the fall, you could easily become an ardent hunter in the spring.

One reason casual observers are unfamiliar with the American woodcock is the secretive nature of the bird. Migrating and feeding—and obviously mating—at night, the woodcock spends the daylight hours resting in locales that most people, short of hunters, won't normally hike through: low, wet, muddy areas near to alders or young aspen stands—the lowlands of the uplands, if you will. As a result, the woodcock is not a bird you will commonly see strutting in a field like a wild turkey, swimming on a pond like a Canada goose, or announcing its presence with the cackling authority of a pheasant. Moreover, it's a tiny bird, rarely weighing as much as half a pound.

The bird's penchant for wet areas is understandable once you understand its history and physiology. The woodcock is a migrant, once a shorebird, belonging to the same family as curlews and sandpipers and the same subfamily as snipes. It's plump, with spindly legs and a long, pointy bill with which it probes in the mud for grubs.

The bill is only one feature of its anatomy, which is a marvel of selective adaptation, from its forest floor–like coloring, to its *big* eyes designed to take in maximum light and let the bird see better when it's most active; to its inverted brain, unique among birds, which made room in its cranium for those large eyes. You can see a stylized carving of a woodcock, much larger than life, in the display of Native American carver "Smokey" Joe Jackson at the Chippewa Nature Center's museum.

For as secretive and solitary as the woodcock is most of the time, the male certainly changes character in spring when he seeks females with which to mate. To begin with, he prefers to lure them to nice, open fields near to where he'd spend most of his days. Second, he puts on an elaborate flight, or dance, accompanying himself with several clearly identifiable songs. Finally, he's been known to perform his flights on a nightly basis from as early as mid-March to as late as early June. The most comfortable viewing conditions usually occur from late April to mid-May.

In order to observe his dance, you need to get to an open field near low-lying woodlands. His flights begin when daylight drops to that mystical level between dusk and dark. Time yourself to get to the field at least half an hour before. Since you will be trying to see a flying shadow, sit on the eastern side of the field and look to the west. This will let you utilize the last available sunlight as a backdrop instead of straining your eyes against the darkness of the eastern sky.

You'll know if a bird intends to dance that night because long before he begins his flights, he'll *peent*. This is the first of his sounds. It sounds like one *beep* from the cartoon Road Runner, or as if the woodcock were giving somebody a raspberry. In the "Sky Dance" essay in *A Sand County Almanac*, Aldo Leopold says that the peent is similar to the summer call of a nighthawk. If darkness starts to descend and you don't hear any peenting, you can bet that the field hasn't yet been claimed by any suitor.

The woodcock will keep up this peenting, sometimes as much as thirty-five or forty times a minute, until the light intensity has dropped to a point where he's satisfied and will begin a flight. He quits peenting just before takeoff. When you hear the whistling of his wings, scan the horizon above the tree line for the silhouette of a half-pound bird with a thin, pointed beak as it traces a wide circle over the field. Basically, you need to use your ears to guide your eyes.

Steadily the woodcock will climb, and he will slowly tighten the circle. As he nears the apex of his flight, sometimes as high as 200 feet, he will change his song to a rich, melodic, bubbling tune that Leopold describes as "liquid warbling." At the apex, he will stop singing, set his wings, and drop with a bit of a wobble, like a parachutist aiming for a spot on a football field. He's likely to land very close to the spot from which he launched himself a minute earlier.

Back on the ground, he'll repeat things, starting with a series of peents.

I used to think biologists were being purposely deceptive or just unfriendly when they wouldn't reveal any specific locations for observing the woodcock dances. But I found out, as you will too, that the textbook description of the area—an open field near a wet upland—is about as specific as you can get because the birds apparently have read the textbook. These simple directions apply statewide.

If you're at all uncertain about your ability to find such an area or about what the bird might sound like, arrange to join one of the woodcock walks many of the nature centers hold. (Several of the Huron-Clinton Metroparks, by the way, sponsor such guided trips. "Dance of the Timberdoodle" they're called, "timberdoodle" being one of the pet names that have been given to this little bird that can impassion hunters twice a year.) Such a start just might get you hooked, and it won't take long before you realize why for some of us, nothing better affirms life cycles than the first peent of spring.

The Wetlands area has an interesting, if brief, history. The state of Michigan has a Wetland Protection Act, which basically requires developers to replace any wetlands they destroy during the construction of their projects. The Chippewa Nature Center was trying to figure out how to develop a recently acquired parcel on its southern edge while at the same time the developer of a shopping mall north of Midland was facing the DNR and the U.S. Environmental Protection Agency's requirement that he replace the wetlands that he had destroyed. Timing is everything, the people at the center say, and the three basins were dug here and their topsoil removed. They were then filled with muck—wetlands pudding, if you will—hauled from the mall construction site.

So, what you are looking at is not a natural wetland, but it is being managed to allow for its natural development.

How to get there: In Midland County, from I-75, take exit 162 west onto US 10. Eleven miles later, take the US 10 Business loop exit. Follow Business 10 for four miles through Midland to

The dead-leaf pattern of a woodcock makes it almost invisible until you're right upon it, then it zigzags off with whistling wings

Cronkright (Poseyville Road). Turn left onto Cronkright, drive over the bridge to St. Charles Street, turn right, and follow the signs for three miles to the center.

General information: The Chippewa Nature Center is open year-round. Trails are open from dawn to dusk for hiking and cross-country skiing, although trails aren't groomed in winter. Bikes are not allowed on the trails. Neither are pets or smoking. Permanent hours have been established for the visitor center: Monday to Friday, 8:00 A.M. to 5:00 P.M.; Saturday, 9:00 A.M. to 5:00 p.m; Sunday, 1:00 to 5:00 P.M.

For brochures, schedules of upcoming programs, and information on membership in this nonprofit educational organization, write Chippewa Nature Center, 400 South Badour Road, Midland, MI 48640; 517-631-0830.

2

Southwest

E. GENEVIEVE GILLETTE NATURE CENTER

Nestled among the sand dunes, the Gillette Nature Center is a wonderful attraction, offering both education and entertainment. Situated as it is in the middle of the P. J. Hoffmaster State Park, which adjoins over two miles of Lake Michigan shoreline, and with three other state parks within easy striking distances, there is a temptation to treat it as an overnight destination and stick around for a legendary Lake Michigan sunset.

It's possible to feel totally isolated, even if you're within a shout and a half of hundreds of people. Try pulling up to the visitors center after closing time on a chilly, rainy, midweek evening early in spring. On your hike over the dune, the saturated yet resilient boardwalk will absorb your footbeats until the damp beach takes over. There Lake Michigan will greet you while some indignant gulls bristle at your intrusion.

If you're smart, or prepared, or at least realistic about your physical conditioning, you'll hike down to the beach first before returning to try the Dune Climb Stairway. The reason is simple.

The stairs climb to about 190 feet above the lake. Your return trip is a simple downhill stair-stepping excursion. If you save the beach for second, you'll have an uphill battle for the last leg of your hike. Of course, you can avoid all the strategy here and spend enough time at each vantage to recoup whatever strength you need to press on.

No doubt, though, you'll want to take both five-minute hikes, to the beach and up the dune. That way, you'll get to see things from two vastly different perspectives.

But if you leave the area with only those two vistas in your memory, you're missing half the allure of the E. Genevieve Gillette Nature Center. So check into one of the 333 modern campsites at Hoffmaster State Park and come back in the morning.

Opened in 1976, the center is named after a philanthropist and pioneer in Michigan conservation. Born in 1898, Ms. Gillette became a landscape architect after graduating from Michigan State University when it was still known as Michigan Agricultural College. She is credited with the creation of the Michigan state park system and for playing a major role in establishing Sleeping Bear Dunes National Lakeshore and Porcupine Mountains State Park. When she died in 1986, she left her entire estate for the purpose of acquiring "a scenic site to give to the people of Michigan." In 1988, the money was used to purchase a huge chunk of what is now Thompson's Harbor Natural Area in northeastern Michigan.

The nature center building is impressive in its own right, with an aluminum roof rising modestly above the wooden walkway from the parking area. The building must remain modest, you see, for in no way can it compete with the majestic dune towering behind it.

Obviously, dunes were on the mind of the center's architects as they will be on yours during your visit, as well they should be. Michigan's Sand Dune Interpretive Center is housed in the

Gillette Nature Center, and dune information is the major focus of the upper portion of the building. On the grand scale, the dunes along Michigan's west coast are the world's largest accumulation of sand dunes along a body of fresh water. On a smaller scale, each dune is a delicate microcosm that follows a clear pattern of development and plant succession.

Step inside to learn about the life of the mounds of sand and grass and trees that you traversed the night before. Find out about the four zones of a dune: beach, foredune, trough, and backdune, each represented by its own display, which is rotated to reveal the appropriate season. You'll learn that certain trees, the cottonwood and sand cherry for instance, grow on foredunes and that backdunes contain overlapping groups of hardwoods; about the sensitive nature of dunes and the grasses, which in turn will help you to better understand the raison d'être for the boardwalks over the dunes.

Take time out to enter the eighty-two-seat theater for the multi-image slide show about dune ecology and the Great Lakes.

Downstairs, you'll find a feature that's set up for organized groups as well as individuals. "Kids who have been here before," said the late Sandy McBeath, the park interpreter in charge of the Dune Interpretive Center, "will rush downstairs to the hands-on classroom to see what's new."

Those kids might have to deal with adult elbows if the grown-ups get much of a taste of what's down there. Certainly, interpreters run student groups through specific lessons. And live "dune critters" are displayed when appropriate – snakes, frogs, and other pond animals. But be sure to work your way in around the table where you can check out the microscope slides of various animal and plant features. You'll be able to examine things like a grouse feather, wild carrot seed, moss, fern, and lichen. Don't overlook the dragonfly wing which, under magnification, resembles unstained panels of stained glass.

All this is just the beginning.

Throughout the 1,100-acre park, over ten miles of trails offer hikers a variety of choices. For example, wise planning for the park resulted in the camping area being separated from the beach day-use area, which in turn is separate from the nature center. Yet it's possible to take a series of trails and meander from the campground to the beach or to the nature center. Or you can reach the shoreline from any of the areas and hike to another area or to the trails near the park's borders.

Depending on your location in the park, the time of day, and the time of year, you may see many of the animals common to Michigan's woods and shorelines: white-tailed deer, raccoons, squirrels, upland birds and songbirds, and shoreline and aquatic birds. If the wind is right, you may even see hawks soaring on the air currents that sweep from the dunes. And you'll realize why Michigan's west coast appeals to hang-gliders.

Spring is wildflower time at Hoffmaster. Such a variety of flowers bloom here that you can pick up information sheets at the nature center and know what to expect to see at various times of the year, and where. Some of the dominant species include jack-in-the-pulpit, wild columbine, trailing arbutus, pink lady's slipper, and wild lily of the valley. McBeath also mentions that Pitcher's thistle is abundant in the park.

No doubt about it, though, the trillium is the drawing card here. This early spring bloomer has even earned its own festival, held on Mother's Day Weekend each year. The three large white petals that clearly identify the large-flowered trillium turn pink with age. You can discover them throughout the park along designated trails.

In winter, a marked three-mile trail is maintained for cross-country skiers of intermediate skill. Snowshoers are also welcome to traipse through the park. Other vehicles such as snow-mobiles, bicycles, and off-road vehicles, however, are not allowed off paved park roads.

How to get there: In Muskegon County, from US 31, take exit 4 to the west, onto Pontaluna Road. Head down Pontaluna about three miles to the P. J. Hoffmaster State Park entrance.

General information: The state park is open year-round from 8:00 A.M. to 10:00 P.M. The nature center is open year-round with seasonal hours. It's closed on Mondays. A motor vehicle permit is required for entry.

Throughout the year, special lectures, guided hikes, and other programs are held through the nature center. For more information on these and the current hours, call 616-798-3573.

For maps, brochures, and park information, contact the Park Manager, P. J. Hoffmaster State Park, 6585 Lake Harbor Road, Muskegon, MI 49441; 616-798-3711.

WOLF LAKE STATE FISH HATCHERY

While the state currently operates six fish hatcheries for raising game fish to be released into Michigan's lakes and rivers, the Wolf Lake Hatchery is the biggest, incubating as many as 70 million walleye eggs a year. What makes Wolf Lake a special attraction, however, is the fact that it is the hatchery that houses the Michigan Fisheries Interpretive Center.

This is one of those spots that you wouldn't drive out of your way to visit but you don't want to pass up if you are in the area. The center is well worth the ten-minute drive from Kalamazoo and the hour or so that you'll spend there. Even if you have never baited a hook or wet a line yourself, you can't help but learn some intriguing facts about the state, its waters, its fish, and both the people who enjoy them recreationally and those who work to improve them.

The Great Lakes comprise an area of over 95,000 square miles. As the "Great Lakes State," Michigan has seen much of its history develop because of the lakes. And fishing plays an important part in Michigan's heritage as well as in its economy and natural history.

The Michigan Fisheries Interpretive Center addresses all these aspects of fishing in the Great Lakes area, and more. It covers 7,000 square feet, including the lobby, a ninety-two-seat auditorium, and the Michigan Room, which contains several displays.

To begin with, each hatchery "specializes" in a species that it rears. Until recently, all the steelhead planted in the state came from Wolf Lake. Its other primary species is the chinook salmon. Therefore, when visitors to the hatchery take a walk on the floating docks over the show pond, they can relish a close-up view of some massive fish that would, under different circumstances, make anglers quiver and drool.

Inside the center itself, anglers can also drool over the display of plaques describing forty-six state record fish, each telling how big the fish was, who caught it, and where it was caught— the kind of information that makes anglers' heads spin and of which their dreams are made. On the walls mounted specimens of fish are grouped by their common family names.

A real pleaser is the giant model of a fish and its anatomy, kind of like an ichthyological version of that "Visible Man" plastic model that a generation of children once found beneath their Christmas trees. Also on display are 3-D models of each of the five Great Lakes, where you'll learn that the name for both the lake and the state comes from the Ojibwa term *Michigama*, meaning "great or large lake." And in the Michigan Room, dioramas give an up-close view of four major types of fish habitats found in lakes and streams, plus the typical inhabitants of each.

If you appreciate craftsmanship on a grand scale, you will enjoy the Au Sable riverboat on display. This type of boat is a classic, a favorite during the golden age of trout fishing on the Au Sable river, clear on the other side of the state. Some guides still use the riverboats, and some people use them on other streams, but no attempt to examine the history of fishing in Michigan would be complete without an Au Sable riverboat.

If you appreciate craftsmanship on a smaller scale, then you'll enjoy the display of antique fishing tackle and lures.

In the auditorium, a ten-minute, multi-projection slide show about Michigan's DNR Fisheries Division is shown, according to employees, "on demand." Also, tours for school children or other groups are easily arranged.

How to get there: In Van Buren County, from US 131 west of Kalamazoo take exit 38B west onto M-43. Follow M-43 for six miles until you reach Hatchery Road. The hatchery is on the south side of M-43.

General information: Admission to the center is free. Hours vary according to the day and season.

For more information or to schedule a group tour, contact the Wolf Lake State Fish Hatchery 34270 C.R. 652, Mattawan, MI 49701; 616-668-2876.

WARREN DUNES STATE PARK

With daylight taking only a timid footstep into the near-blizzard of an early January morning, the visitor to Warren Dunes needs to use his imagination in several ways. First, of course, is to guess correctly the location of the park road, for either the snowplows haven't awakened yet, or they have and it doesn't matter. Next is to imagine sunnier days and more than just one vehicle roaming the area as Warren Dunes assumes its normal position near the top of the "most used state parks" list. Finally, as the vehicle rolls to a stop at the end of the parking area, with a frozen Lake Michigan on the left and a living mound of sand blanketed in snow to the right, imagination quickly sparks the realization of the strength of Warren Dunes as a place to visit.

This is the busiest state park, probably because it offers the complete package: lake, beach, and "dunal" experience all within a couple miles of the interstate highway. Easy access also makes this park a desirable stopping spot for visitors from other states who enter at Michigan's southwestern corner. The traveler who may be in a hurry to touch base with nature will find his needs answered at Warren Dunes, and so will the timid hiker.

Unlike the great dune at Sleeping Bear Dunes National Seashore, from whose perch a visitor still has to hike over a mile and descend about 1,000 feet to get to Lake Michigan in the distance, the Great Warren Dune is much more manageable. To begin with, the parking lot offers a choice: turn one way, and you're basically walking the beach; turn the other, and you begin your ascent of the dunes.

Things are in smaller scale here, but again, the lake is the same and the dune, though less massive, is a bona fide dune, so popular that the Mount Randall area here has been closed to visitors. The mount, with its spectacular view of the lake, has attracted lots of human foot traffic. Feet cause erosion and prevent critical dune vegetation from taking hold. As a result, the western edge of the dune has been worn to the point of instability and the prevailing west winds are helping it to creep eastward.

The mile-long Warren Dunes Nature Trail begins in the parking lot near the beach and the base of the dunes. Expect to see various types of vegetation, evidence that the dunes are in various stages of development.

Both the smaller size of this dune area and its location will appeal to the reluctant hiker. It's impossible to get lost here. No, check that—someone is bound to prove me wrong. Put it like this: someone unfamiliar with the area can hike with confidence if he remembers his compass. How's that? Simple. The park is located in a narrow strip, only about a mile wide, bounded by the lake on one side and Red Arrow Highway on the other. In the unlikely event that you get twisted around, all you have to do is to head west until you hit big water or head east until you hit blacktop. In fact, along the exit from I-94, only a small fence, tiny in juxtaposition, warns the backdune against merging with the highway.

How to get there: In Berrien County, from I-94, take exit 16 onto Red Arrow Highway. Follow that road southwest for about two miles to the park entrance.

General information: For those interested in making this park an overnight destination, it is one of several state parks that offers mini-cabins in addition to modern campsites.

Also, only a few miles down the road, Warren Woods Natural Area offers 311 acres of pristine beech-maple forest, home to many species of warblers and thrushes as well as pileated woodpeckers and barred owls.

A motor vehicle permit is required for all vehicles entering either park, and separate fees are charged for campsites at Warren Dunes.

For more information on either park, contact the park manager at Warren Dunes State Park, Red Arrow Highway, Sawyer, MI 49125; 616-426-4013.

KELLOGG BIRD SANCTUARY

If hope for wild things is best nurtured through education of the masses, then the Kellogg Bird Sanctuary is a vibrant reminder that hope is not lost. If the name sounds familiar, you've guessed correctly. The Kellogg Bird Sanctuary, Biological Station, Experimental Forest and Farm—a 3,600-acre complex—were developed by W. K. Kellogg, who, in partnership with his brother, made nearby Battle Creek famous with his cereal company. And Kellogg is also a name prominent in Michigan philanthropy.

In the mid-1920s, influenced by some of the pioneers in the

emerging field of wildlife conservation and game management, Kellogg established his own project on beautiful Wintergreen Lake, fourteen miles northwest of Battle Creek. He bought the neglected farmland and had it restored and developed as a bird sanctuary, primarily for waterfowl. This proved to be a fortuitous move, for research eventually showed that Wintergreen Lake sits at the crossroads of three major bird migration routes.

By 1928, Kellogg had deeded the Sanctuary and Experimental Farm to what is now Michigan State University. The first two students began working there in 1930. Also, since the sanctuary's inception the public has been encouraged to visit. So it truly has developed as a spot where education, thus hope, can flourish.

Nowadays, with geese so plentiful they are considered nuisances in many areas of the state, it may be hard to believe that in the 1920s Canada geese only migrated through Michigan — none nested here. As a result, they were one of the early species that Kellogg hoped to attract. That attraction has been completely successful as you can easily see, especially in the fall of the year.

Human traffic at the sanctuary peaks about the same time as the waterfowl traffic in fall, the last two weeks in October and first week in November. Visitors can see upward of 5,000 Canada geese, many of the native duck species, and even some swans. Migration, of course, plays a part in these numbers. So does hunting. You see, the birds are no dummies, and they will naturally congregate in spots like the sanctuary when they feel too much pressure from nearby hunters.

Since 1986, the sanctuary has been taking part in a program to reintroduce the magnificent trumpeter swan to Michigan, from which it had been extirpated since the 1880s. The goal of this program is to populate the wilds with 200 birds by the year 2000. At the sanctuary, eggs gathered from other spots in the U.S. were incubated and hatched. The young swans, or *cygnets,* were raised until they matured at two years of age. Each year for three years, forty birds were released on selected wetlands throughout the state. If you're lucky during your visit, you'll hear the wonderful call that has earned the trumpeter its name.

To do this, take a stroll along the self-guiding trail. It's only about three-quarters of a mile long, but you'll want to take your time at each of the numbered stops, so allow at least an hour. A pamphlet you can pick up at the welcoming center/gift shop will acquaint you with the types of animals you should see at various spots along the way.

Although waterfowl are the main draw here, a rare feature of the sanctuary is its "Birds of Prey" display. While the other birds are free to come and go as they please, these birds are, understandably, caged. While this treatment may play into a negative "zoo mentality," realize that these are injured birds; some are being rehabilitated; others too badly hurt to survive in the wild have become permanent residents.

The thing that makes Kellogg a sanctuary for humans as well as birds is its setting. The grounds are expansive and well maintained. Plus they're tucked far enough away from major highways so that the drone of traffic doesn't interfere with the experience. Wintergreen Lake and its waterfowl lagoon sit at

A trumpeter swan and cygnets searching for breakfast

the base of a small hill below the welcome center. In summer, the surrounding vegetation is lush, the tranquil paddling of the waterfowl equally tranquilizing—*serenity* is a word that slips in and makes itself at home. Even when one of the swans or geese removes its cloak of grace and clambers from the water to become land-borne, the overall effect is still calming as you get to observe the animal's behavior when it's not under stress: nature at ease.

Different patches on the grounds are used for experimental habitat-improvement projects. For example, one section has been dedicated as a prairie restoration project. And the Experimental Forest itself, near the junction of 42nd Street and M-89 a few miles from the Bird Sanctuary, contains a large variety of tree species for the skier or hiker who wants to venture beyond the short loops onto the forest's twenty-five miles of ungroomed trails and firebreaks.

The Kellogg Bird Sanctuary can also provide more information about its natural and man-honed features than you may be ready to absorb all at once. That's OK, because the sanctuary is a spot to which you'll want to return again and again.

How to get there: In Kalamazoo County, imagine, in rough form, a squat triangle with Kalamazoo and Battle Creek at either end of a baseline along I-94. The Kellogg Bird Sanctuary is located at the triangle's apex to the north, about a ten-mile drive from I-94. Take exit 95 (Helmer Road) north to Dickman Road. Turn west (left) onto Dickman, which will become M-96 (the *state highway*, not the interstate). Drive past the Fort Custer Recreation Area, across the Kalamazoo River, and into the hamlet of Augusta. Turn north onto Webster, which, upon leaving town, becomes 42nd Street. Take 42nd to M-89 and turn west. About a mile down the road, turn north on 40th Street. Take that to "C" Avenue. The route is well marked with signs for the sanctuary.

General information: The sanctuary is open daily throughout the year. Hours change according to seasons and available sunlight. A nominal admission is charged.

For specifics, contact the Kellogg Bird Sanctuary, 12685 East "C" Avenue, Augusta, MI 49012; 616-671-2510.

BERNARD W. BAKER SANCTUARY

With my approach, a pair of mallards flush from the protection of the marsh. A groundhog lazily climbs a tree trunk until it notices me, drops to the ground, and scatters away with a speed I didn't realize that species possessed. As I step toward the kiosk that explains the Iva Doty Flower Trail, part of the sanctuary, a cock pheasant cackles, defiantly challenging my decision to explore.

Technically, the Doty Trail sits "on" the Baker Sanctuary. The land is part of the sanctuary proper, but the care and maintenance of the trail falls to the hands of the Doty Native Flower Garden Association.

I always feel a sense of "right" when my feet tread a boardwalk shielding sensitive land I would otherwise trample — although in this case I think the boardwalk has also been installed to prevent soakers as people traverse the property during times of spongy soil and puddles from spring runoff.

Pausing along the boardwalk I notice three mallards overhead. From behind, a hen pheasant startles, as always, with her takeoff. She encourages the cock to join her, and he flushes far beyond the dogwood that marks the eastern boundary of the sanctuary.

A second hen takes flight, not fifteen feet from where I stand. A muskrat house in the marsh prompts me to muse whether he is lulled by the traffic on I-69. I recognize skunk cabbage and jack-in-the-pulpit among the dozen or so flower species that have poked their heads into the fresh air of spring. Deer tracks and rabbit droppings bespeak the presence of yet more animals.

I require only one more sign for the experience to be complete — and there it is. Whitewashing various leaves beside the trail, half-dollar-sized bird droppings indicate the sanctuary is frequented by my favorite harbinger of spring, the American woodcock.

A glorious experience even without the cranes.

Encompassing about 900 acres, the Bernard W. Baker Sanctuary is one of the two top spots for viewing sandhill cranes in southern Michigan. Even in 1941, at the time Bernard W. Baker donated the original 491 acres to the Michigan Audubon Society, this spot was a primary nesting areas for sandhill cranes. Much of the development of the sanctuary has been undertaken in an effort to benefit these large, storklike birds.

For example, the sanctuary abuts an additional 131-acre tract owned by the Kiwanis Club of Battle Creek. In 1961, the two groups joined forces to dam Big Marsh Lake, which created more wetland and nesting areas for the cranes. That wetland now covers nearly 200 acres, and all told, about 75 percent of the sanctuary is under standing water at least part of the year. This creates an appealing habitat for many species of waterfowl and water mammals. Other animals are attracted by the fact that at least remnants of virtually every type of habitat found in southern Michigan are sprinkled throughout the sanctuary.

Sad to say, disrespect for the natural features — what Mike Boyce, the current resident manager, kindly refers to as "pilfering" — has caused officials to close all trails with the exception of the Doty Trail. People do pick the wildflowers although that is illegal. One trail used to abound with wild orchids. But officials have responded to the "pilfering" by letting that trail grow over. Same thing with another that led back to a sensitive crane nesting area. As of this writing, therefore, if visitors want to hike beyond the loop on the Doty Trail, they have to plan their visit for a time when the Kiwanis land is open to the public. That's usually on weekends during the summer and in October and November.

The Kiwanis property offers the best view of the cranes, however. The best time of year to see them is in the fall as they stage, or assemble, for their southern migration.

In the fall of 1993, Boyce observed a maximum of 1,200 cranes at one time assembled in the marsh. They'd lift off together in smaller groups, get into their pinwheel formation, and head higher and higher till their squeaky gate–sounding "Kawrook" could no longer be heard.

While in the fall the cranes certainly demand your attention, in spring start looking also for some trumpeter swans. They've been released in the sanctuary, have nested there the last few years, and have raised some young. So it's a fair bet that they will return.

How to get there: In Calhoun County, from I-94, take exit 108 to I-69, north toward Lansing. After only a few miles, take exit 42 west onto North Drive (Gorsline Road). Very quickly, you'll need to make a right turn to head north on 16 Mile Road for about

---

BE PREPARED

Even though you'll be less than a mile from a major interstate, you'll want to take along three items as you hike along the Doty Trail: waterproof boots, insect repellent, and a compass. The first two are self-explanatory, considering that 75 percent of the property is wet. The third you will want if you plan to complete the loop at the end of the trail. You'll find the compass handy should you somehow get off the trail that's maintained by humans and slip onto a game trail worn thin by deer. That loop extends onto a point which, in turn, gives way to marshlands. Lots of deer crisscross that point. It's easy to get onto the wrong trail. Trust me.

two miles. Take the left branch of the Y in the road to get onto Junction Road. (Taking the right will head you down Garfield Road.) About a quarter mile ahead on the left is the driveway for the sanctuary.

General information: The Baker Sanctuary is open year-round. There is no charge for admission.

For informative brochures, write to: Baker Sanctuary Resident Manager, 21145 15 Mile Road, Bellevue, MI 49201.

Also, try contacting Mike Boyce at the Michigan Audubon Society, 6011 West St. Joseph, Suite 403, P.O. Box 80527, Lansing, MI 48908-0527; 517-886-9144.

YANKEE SPRINGS RECREATION AREA

Long before and long after a New Englander carved two words into the side of an oak tree—"Yankee Springs"—this area has remained an important and intriguing locale, playing a historical and a recreational role in the lives of Michigan's people. Hunting grounds of the Algonquian Indians, stagecoach station along the Indian trail halfway between Grand Rapids and Kalamazoo, an area devastated by farmers then resurrected and rehabilitated by the federal government, this spot brims with legend, history, and possibility.

Currently, the Yankee Springs Recreation Area covers over 5,000 acres and adjoins the 15,000-acre Barry State Game Area, creating over 20,000 acres of possibility.

As with most places in Michigan, much of the natural appeal of Yankee Springs can be attributed to the "facelift" the land was given by the glaciers thousands of years ago. One of the most popular features is the overlook at Graves Hill, a glacial moraine, basically the pile of debris created by the glacier as it melted but before it began to retreat. From the vantage of the Graves Hill Overlook, you can view much of the recreation area. Other moraines in the area add to its rugged quality.

Other popular features caused by the glaciers are the "Devil's Soupbowls," old, dried-out kettle lake formations that, as their name suggests, appear to be large bowls beside a ridge. The larger of the two is more than 100 feet deep and about 900 feet across. They are conveniently located about a quarter mile from the Graves Hill Overlook. You can reach the Soupbowls by car via the graded dirt road leading north from Gun Lake Road. The road can get rough, but it's passable. Plus you might see some wildlife here.

Fran Brown, the park secretary at Yankee Springs, gave me the usual rundown of animals you can expect to see here: rabbit, ruffed grouse, squirrels, geese, ducks, wild turkey, hawks, songbirds, and deer. "There's lots of deer," she said. "That's the biggest thing."

Almost on cue, the deer began showing up. Mind you, I visited the area in early April during a light mist. As a result, very few people had been prowling the woods. But in my short drive from the turnoff in the dirt road that leads up to Graves Hill, I spotted nine deer. And I wasn't being particularly observant, wasn't driving particularly slowly, wasn't trying very hard. Once again, the concept was hammered home that if you want to see wildlife, spring is the best time to do it, just as the animals begin moving about and before too many people do.

You can also reach Graves Hill and the Soupbowls by some of the area's fifteen plus miles of designated hiking trails. Remember, the area is loaded with moraines, and moraines are hills, so if you decide to hike, choose a route that you are physically ready to handle. To put it another way, consider the fact that some of the same trails (about ten miles) are groomed in winter for cross-country skiing. And the pamphlet distributed at the state park headquarters reads, "Even though all trails are classed 'most difficult,' there is ample room for first timers." Then again, it finishes with "if in doubt, take off the skis and walk the short distance to the bottom." Expect hilly terrain. Of course, hikers, skiers, and snowshoers are free to traipse over whatever real estate they choose throughout the entire rec area.

Snowmobilers, however, must remain on the designated snowmobile trail or on roads maintained for motorized vehicles. Motorcycles and ATVs must remain on roads only. Mountain bikes, like snowmobiles, may be operated only on the designated trail. And the mountain bike trail is separate from the hiking trails.

With a trailhead at Deep Lake on the eastern edge of the recreation area, the mountain bike trail includes loops that total nearly twelve miles. It starts out kindly, rolling over flat land to get you warmed up. Eventually it heads over some of the most rugged hills in the area, through tough sand pockets, and across a creek. It skirts the rim of the Soupbowls, and from there you can jump onto the gravel road to the Graves Hill Overlook, should you choose.

That's not to say that the trails constantly head up and down. As a matter of fact, some of the trails move through low bog areas, one of which is so low that a boardwalk has been constructed so cyclists can pedal through. Incidentally, in spring, this is a good place to see marsh wildflowers.

Backpackers will be happy to note that the North Country Trail, the National Park Service route that heads across the northern tier of states, can be joined at a trailhead on the southeast edge of the rec area along Yankee Springs Road south of Gun Lake Road.

There's even something for horseback riders at Yankee Springs. Not far from the North Country trailhead, just south of Duffy Road, they'll find a horseback campground and two five-mile loops for riding. The northern loop passes alongside a plantation of tall pines, a remnant of the days of the CCC camps of the 1930s. From that loop, riders can connect to an eight-mile

White-tailed deer can be seen most frequently at dawn and dusk

loop in the Barry State Game Area. That loop, however, is closed during hunting season, roughly October 1 to January 1, but it's best to double-check with DNR personnel before heading across Yankee Springs/Morris Road. Within the rec area, horses must remain on designated trails. They may not be ridden on roads maintained by the DNR. They are, however, allowed on county roads.

Nonequestrian campers have a choice of camping styles at Yankee Springs. There's a modern campground at Gun Lake and rustic camping at Deep Lake. Long Lake features organizational camping for tents only. And the cabins at both the Chief Noonday and Long Lake Outdoor Centers are available year-round, both large cabins for large groups and frontier cabins for smaller groups. Advance reservations are recommended for all seasons, and reservations for November through March can be made two years in advance. Some of the groomed ski trails pass by the Long Lake cabins, making a tempting winter getaway.

Folks who like big water will appreciate Gun Lake's modern boat launch, bathhouse and beach, day-use area, and picnic shelter. Those who like smaller waters will find access sites at seven other lakes within the rec area proper: Baker, Payne, Chief Noonday, Long, McDonald, Deep, and Hall. Hall Lake is pretty heavily fished.

Car-top boaters and canoeists who prefer even more seclusion might travel down Yankee Springs/Morris Road about five miles south of Gun Lake Road to Guernsey Lake Road. Turn west and enjoy the drive. Guernsey Lake has been designated a "Natural Beauty Road," and as a result must be maintained in its present state. Trees may not be cut, and the road may not be widened. The north side cradles hardwoods like maple and oak. Soon, the south side gives way to a bog rimmed with osier.

About 2.5 miles after turning, you'll see a small spot where you can gain access to the lake on the north side. You can launch here and park along the road. The big lake is Fish Lake, and channels from it lead to Lime and Horseshoe Lakes as well as Mill Pond. Rising from the marshy shorelines, the land quickly becomes hills of mature hardwoods. The restrictions of the boat launch and the minimal development on these lakes just about guarantee you will have to share your cruise only with natural denizens such as mallards and wood ducks and an occasional great blue heron as it "awwk-awwks" away after detecting you.

For even more seclusion, enter the creek on the south side of Guernsey Lake Road and paddle into Tamarack Lake. So far the land has not been developed. State land ends north of the lake, but as long as you enter by water only – via the creek – you are legal.

If you prefer the sounds of nature over the sounds of humans, these southernmost spots may best suit you and your paddling needs.

How to get there: From US 131 in Allegan County, take exit 61. Head east and follow the signs for eight miles to the Yankee Springs Recreation Area headquarters (located in Barry County). *General information:* Yankee Springs is administered by the Parks Division of the DNR. A motor vehicle permit is required for entry. And the various camping options require varying fees.

Pamphlets and maps are available for mountain biking and horse riding trails, cabin rental, cross-country ski trails, and the rec area in general. Contact Yankee Springs Recreation Area, 2104 Gun Lake Road, Middleville, MI 49333; 616-795-9081.

MAPLE RIVER STATE GAME AREA

It's easy to catch a glimpse of migrating birds, if you are in the right place at the right time, and the Maple River flooding along US 27 is a prime place. Spring, when birds are in their colorful breeding plumage, and fall, when the sun's descent in the southern sky urges them on, are the times.

"In early to mid-March the swans will come through," says wildlife biologist Al Stewart. "Tundra swans. They're the last to filter through in the fall and the first to return."

The spring migration runs from March to May; the fall migration, from September to November. A large population of birds maintains residence at this flooding year-round. One reason this area gets so much feathered traffic is its size. Maple River is the "largest wetland complex of its type in mid-Michigan," says

Stewart, adding that it contains about "two thousand wetland acres. That tends to concentrate the birds."

The major factor that would tend to concentrate people is the area's location, smack dab along a major highway. A visitor can literally turn off the highway right into the parking area. Access is that easy, making for a relatively painless field trip. Recently built, a barrier-free hunting/observation blind offers access to even more people. The project earned the Teddy Roosevelt Conservation Award.

On the north edge of the game area, along Taft Road, with "room to experiment," the DNR has constructed "pair bonding" ponds for waterfowl, small irregularly shaped man-made ponds designed to resemble the natural prairie potholes in other parts of the country. Nearby the department has planted switchgrass, a native prairie-type grass that is favorable nesting habitat for the wildfowl and upland birds alike.

"My job at this area is like it is at all areas," says Stewart. "To be as diversified as I can so that a wide variety of wildlife benefits from it."

Judging from the tracks of a massive deer and the short, teasing flights of two, spring-feisty cock pheasants, that diversity in management plan is paying off.

Actually, the area exists as it does primarily as a result of the attempts of early farmers to raise crops along the river's floodplain. They built dikes to keep the water out of their fields. When the state bought the property, it used the dikes to keep the water in, not out.

"The floodplain provides us with free water in spring, and in fall we can pump it in, too, if we need to," says Stewart.

While the hand of man cannot be denied here, nature is clearly the main attraction. From the fifteen-foot-tall observation deck, a short half-mile hike from the parking lot, you can look back to see the heron rookery. Dozens of ducks of several species rest in the numerous ponds and floodings that nearly surround you. And geese, of course. "Usually we have Canada geese, mallards, and wood ducks nesting," says Stewart. "And there are some redheads that nest in here."

To the east an eagle nest looms. You'll know if the bald eagles have returned if you see the "Caution! Do Not Enter" yellow tape that blocks the path along one of the dikes. A couple years ago they were scared off by some birders who ignored the banner.

You can see a lot of ducks in spring, but the vegetation is not pretty—mostly dead, brown cattails. If you get to the barrier-free blind by sunrise, you may hear the result of recent wild turkey plantings gobbling away.

Stewart thinks that spring "would be a neat time to float the river because the water's high." Not to worry, however, for even at high water, the river is slow. This is the body of water that has produced the state record channel catfish, a creature found in slow-moving bodies of water. As a matter of fact, the biggest worry for canoeists would be drifting from the main channel of the river into the floodplain. "But all you have to do is head back to the tree line and you'll be all right," says Stewart.

Throughout the summer, aside from the resident waterfowl, the nesting great blue herons are visible, as well as egrets and coots.

Remember that this area also attracts hunters and that early seasons on teal and geese are sometimes open the first part of September. Stewart recommends a trip to view the fall migration sometime between September 15 and 30, when you can also pick up a jug of cider from a local orchard and luxuriate in the spectacle of the birds as they stage, or assemble, for the next leg of their southern journey.

How to get there: In Gratiot County, about eight miles north of St. Johns, US 27 crosses the Maple River. A parking spot is on the northeast corner of the intersection of the road and the river.

HERON OR CRANE?

There's a simple way to distinguish between these two birds when you just glimpse one behind some cattails or see one fly away without identifying any field marks. A crane will "crane" its neck—will extend its neck—while a heron will fold its neck into an *S*. Also, cranes always stand on the ground, never in trees. As a result, great blue herons will be the big birds you see in giant nests in the trees. Cranes will nest in deep-water marshy areas, often in cattails.

An easily reached attraction for those interested in viewing migrating birds, the Maple River Game Area gets placed in "southwest" for two reasons. First, a look at a map will show that the area strings along, meandering with the river, and most of the area's nearly 10,000 acres fall to the west of US 27, up to the Ionia County line. Second, especially in spring, a glance west across the highway will reveal a vast blue heron rookery; the massive nests in the tops of the bare trees cradle the cranelike birds as they raise their families each spring.

General information: No fees or stickers are required for entrance to the Maple River State Game Area. For a detailed map, contact the Area Wildlife Biologist, Rose Lake Wildlife Office, 8562 East Stoll Road, East Lansing, MI 48823; 517-373-9358.

3

Northeast

THOMPSON'S HARBOR STATE PARK

"This is not what you call prime state park country, but it's good country for wandering around in," says the DNR Parks Division's Jerry Smith, who mapped out most of Thompson's Harbor State Park.

The appeal of the park lies in its remote, mostly undeveloped condition. The land is wild. A few foot trails offer subtle links from roads to more remote areas. A few clearings remain. But for the most part, the land is untamed, second-growth timber interrupted now and then by low lies and swamps. As a result, wildlife abounds, both game species—deer, grouse, rabbit, bobcat, and coyote—as well as nongame—Cooper's hawks, red-shouldered hawks, loons, and bald eagles.

The careful hiker or skier stands a great chance of spotting wildlife at Thompson's Harbor. And if not the animals themselves, certainly their signs are prevalent along the trails. Skiers especially will want to tote guidebooks of animal tracks in order to distinguish among the dozens of tracks they'll see in the snow. Bobcat and coyote tracks are as common as those of white-tailed deer, grouse, and hares. Telltale feathers may indicate where a ruffed grouse lost a struggle with a predator, the mystery of whose tracks you'll have to solve.

This delightfully wild character of the land so close to a highway makes it very attractive to those who crave outdoor adventure not far from the hum of civilization. Only one factor prevents the park from being an overnight destination. No

**You seldom see bobcats because their spotted coats
blend in so well with their surroundings**

campgrounds have yet been built at Thompson's Harbor, and in state parks camping is not allowed anywhere but in developed campsites.

Yet, as state property, the land is available for public use. All roads are closed to motorized vehicles, save for the one leading to the parking spot. The old survey lines, logging roads, and power line corridor can become paths for hikers or skiers willing to break their own trails. Even the cleared trails are not groomed for skiers, so Thompson's Harbor remains a place for escaping the crowds.

As wild as the land is, the trails are not rugged. In fact, with its fairly flat topography, Thompson's Harbor offers hiking and skiing that should be rated "mostly easy." For skiers, the most difficult spots are the sections of loops 1 and 3 that pass along some of the park's seven miles of undeveloped shoreline. There, the wind off Lake Huron builds "snow dunes," and trail breaking and skiing become a little more like work.

This shoreline has been called "the most attractive aspect of the site, undeveloped, remote beauty." And as far back as 1958, the National Park Service rated the Thompson's Harbor shoreline as one of twenty-two in the Great Lakes region worthy of preservation.

Undeveloped and diverse, the shoreline contains marshes, swamps, forests, narrow beaches, limestone points, and an uneven line of sand dunes. The area is also dotted with shallow marl (clay) pools, which are found in only two other Michigan counties.

You'll also notice some unique plant communities. In many spots the sand dunes are covered by wild grass, bearberry, low junipers, and other recumbent plants. Among the hundreds of plant species found throughout the site are the state-threatened Pitcher's thistle and Houghton's goldenrod. A healthy black morel mushroom population also crops up each spring.

OTHER TEMPTING TRAILS

Visitors looking for a little less wilderness but lots of natural beauty nevertheless should head for P. H. Hoeft State Park, about five miles north of Rogers City along US 23. The trail system covers quite a diverse cross section of territory in its total length of 4.5 miles. In the winter, the trails are groomed, offering gentle challenges with only a few, small slopes—no real hills. The sand dunes and Lake Huron adapt their characters to winter, thus providing the unique setting of the Beach Trail. The Nagel Creek Trail runs into the lowlands near the creek where the alert and lucky skier or hiker might see a bald eagle shopping for lunch. Visitors who seek a longer, though no more difficult escape, will take the trail across US 23, following the loop through the hardwoods.

Unlike Thompson's Harbor, Hoeft is a developed state park with campsites, so it can be an overnight destination at any time of the year.

Two more nearby spots, the Ocqueoc Falls Bicentennial Pathway and the Herman Vogler Conservation Area, deserve mention.

The entrance to the Vogler Trail is on Forest Avenue off US 23, about half a mile north of the Rogers City business loop. Also known as the Trout River Trail, this system consists of four main trails and several intersections. Hikers and skiers can just about customize their own daily tours. The trails, nearly five miles in total length, cover a range of land and timber types, from upland hardwoods to cedar swamps. They also cross or otherwise follow the Trout River, its nine-acre flooding, and Hartwick Creek. In winter, skiers will find themselves gliding across snow-covered boardwalks that provide dry footing for hikers at other times of the year. Hit the ski trails early and you might flush a ruffed grouse from its winter roost beneath the snow.

The Ocqueoc Falls Pathway, located between Rogers City and Onaway just off M-68, follows the Ocqueoc River for the outward-bound portion of each of its three loops. The trail is well marked and passes through some nice areas of mature hardwoods and pines. The shortest loop is two and a half miles, the longest, seven, and all three offer more challenging skiing and climbing for the beginner. The skiing and hiking are not difficult, just a bit more vigorous than at the other spots mentioned in this section. All three trails begin by heading in a northeast direction from their start at the parking lot. Their communal final leg marches along the river and up to the largest waterfalls in the Lower Peninsula of Michigan. But don't set your expectations for much more than a six-foot drop. Motorized vehicles are not allowed on these trails, so you shouldn't have to worry about snowmobiles or motorcycles interrupting your peace and quiet.

Of ecological import is the fact that, in addition to the sensitive sand dunes, Thompson's Harbor cradles the world's largest population of the dwarf lake iris, which is listed on both the state and federal threatened species lists. These short-lived tiny purple flowers abound throughout the park to the extent that in springtime the uninformed observer would be hard-pressed to believe they are in any danger at all.

Further development of the park will be determined by the availability of funds. When development does get under way, the park will contain four major zones.

One area, the Environmentally Sensitive Zone, basically follows the shoreline where most of the dwarf lake iris is found.

Another zone, 205 acres near the east end of the park, was designated in 1978 as a Dedicated Natural Area. One of the few sand dune formations found along the Lake Huron shoreline is located within this zone.

How to get there: Along US 23 about thirteen miles south of the blinking light marking the business loop in Rogers City (in Presque Isle County), a brown sign marks the entrance to Thompson's Harbor State Park. Follow the road in for about a mile to the parking area near the trailheads. The three loops offer a total of 6.4 miles of trails for hiking or cross-country skiing.

General information: If you visit during the week, the caretaker at Hoeft State Park should also have maps available for Thompson's Harbor State Park. Or contact the park manager beforehand at Hoeft State Park, US 23 North, Rogers City, MI 49779; 517-734-2543.

You can also call Clear Lake State Park, 517-785-4388.

Also, the Presque Isle County Tourism Council has prepared a free Winter Recreation pamphlet that includes maps of the Hoeft, Ocqueoc Falls, and Vogler trails. To request one, call the council at 800-622-4148.

BLACK MOUNTAIN FOREST RECREATION AREA

Under development only since 1990, the Black Mountain Forest Recreation Area has yet to be adorned with all the amenities planners have envisioned for it. At one moment, DNR representatives gush with the thought that BMFRA "could become a premier mountain biking destination in the Midwest," replete with a big-time luxury lodge. Yet, they also caution, the DNR is still assessing the effects of mountain bikes on the trails. As it stands right now, mountain bikes as well as horses may be ridden on all trails, pathways, and roads not specifically posted as closed to them. Moreover, they may not be ridden off any of these established byways.

That caution should give you an idea of the scope of the area and the mountain itself. For some reason, it strikes me more as a place that commands you to engage in some kind of vehicular activity and not merely hike.

Sure, the BMFRA is open to hunters on foot during open seasons, and campers at the two small state forest campgrounds doubtlessly walk around a bit. But the combination of the trail system, massive real estate comprising the rec area, the openness of the large tracts of mature hardwoods and pines—all of these sing of a place to be enjoyed on the grand scale. Couple that image with the realization that a second system of trails is open to snowmobiles and motorcycles and you'll realize that the BMFRA is not a retreat assuring peace, quiet, and solitude. But it is a great spot for moving around in areas that exist for that purpose but are still in a relatively undeveloped state.

For example, the BMFRA contains about thirty miles of ski trails that are groomed "every day, if possible," says Bob Slater, district manager of the Mackinaw State Forest, which administers the BMFRA.

The trails are marked very well. You can't ski or bike for long without hitting a trail marker with map and directions attached. Slater calls the area "user friendly but somewhat wild." A good example of this would be the spots on the trail that allow beginners to continue along a ridge while advanced skiers take a rugged downhill run and then make the climb back up to the ridge. Slater estimates that about five miles of ski trails are set aside for skate-style skiers and five for advanced skiers. The remaining twenty miles are roughly split between novice and intermediate ratings. The topography ranges from "gently rolling" to "suicidal for the tyro," and the trails cut through a variety of forest types. Along the trails you'll find four warming shelters, three-sided log structures, with grills nearby for building cook fires. These shelters are situated so as to offer a beautiful view of Black Lake, especially at sundown. Plans are also under way to create designated bonfire areas.

Visitors might observe white-tailed deer, coyotes, and turkeys, and Slater says that one plan is to have a local sportsman's group establish a feeding program for the animals in an opening near a novice trail, thus increasing the odds that people will see some wildlife.

Forestry officials continually monitor the use of the area, including the effects of the mountain bikes, to stay within their stated philosophy of "providing as many recreational opportunities as we can until we find there are problems," notes Slater.

The BMFRA could become a jewel in northern Michigan. Just don't expect to have it all to yourself when you get there.

How to get there: Located in Cheboygan and Presque Isle Counties, the BMFRA is just about bisected by the county line. From Onaway, head north on M-211 about six miles until it comes to a T near the Onaway State Park signs. Turn right for about half a mile, then left on County Road 489, which will skirt the east shore of Black Lake for a couple of miles. Stay on 489 until you come to a parking lot on the left. You can also turn left onto Black Mountain Road when it crosses 489. This road will lead to other parking areas in the BMFRA.

General information: The BMFRA remains under the auspices of the DNR's Forest Division, unlike the other rec areas, which belong to the Parks Division. As a result, visitors are not required to have a motor vehicle permit to use the BMFRA.

For a current map of BMFRA, write to the Mackinaw State Forest District Manager, DNR, Box 667, Gaylord, MI 49735.

You can also contact the Rogers City Chamber of Commerce, 209 South Bradley Highway, Rogers City, MI 49779; 800-622-4148.

Or try the Onaway Chamber of Commerce, 310 West State Street, Onaway, MI 49765; 517-733-2874.

SINKHOLES PATHWAY

As they made their retreat from this area tens of thousands of years ago, glaciers left a layer, about 150 feet thick, of sand, clay, and stones covering a bedrock of limestone, which itself extended down several hundred feet. Scattered throughout the limestone, like holes in a piece of swiss cheese, were underground caverns, or hollows. Over the years, water dissolved much of the limestone, thus collapsing the caves and creating the sinkholes. The five sinkholes along this trail are representative of a larger group in this *karst*, or limestone region, which extends to Lake Huron. In addition to sinkholes, a karst will contain abrupt ridges, caverns, and underground streams.

From the vantage offered by your position along the pathway, you can get a bird's-eye view of treetops within and surrounding the holes. Careful, though. Going face-to-face with treetops that should be towering over you may induce a bit of vertigo. Two short loops make up the pathway: a short three-quarter-mile hike, and a longer one of 1.5 miles. Additionally, since the pathway is located in the Mackinaw State Forest, all 2,600 acres in the area are open to the public, and hikers are welcome to set out on their own to explore the area and find, perhaps, some of the other sinkholes located nearby. Dozens of forest trails and logging roads, however, mean that smart hikers will carry both topographic maps and a compass, which they will need if they choose to leave the pathway.

The most dramatic of the holes is the first one. It's the deepest, at 125 feet. Curiously enough, its bottom is about 120 feet lower than the surface waters of Shoepac Lake right across the road. It also has a feature that might make you want to consider visiting the sinkholes late in the afternoon once the skies clear from a day-long rain, and stir-crazy kids have just about done you in.

That first sinkhole has a stairway to its bottom. What a wonderful treat for those kiddies, who probably need to walk carefully to the bottom and then race to the top. They might even be encouraged to include in their laps the one-eighth-mile circular path at the bottom of the sinkhole. After one or two of these enduro races, they should be tuckered out. For an added attraction, tell them they need to count the steps from the top of the pathway to the bottom of the hole. To be extra sure, they should count both on the way up and on the way down. That ought to keep them quiet, too. (Just in case you wonder—or need to send them back for a recount—the total is 237, from the very first step.)

Interestingly enough, Shoepac Lake across the way is also a sinkhole, as are other small lakes in the area. Clay and silt deposits on its bottom, however, act as a drain plug and hold in the water. Shoepac Lake is an active sinkhole, and to the right of the parking area, you can see evidence of the collapses of 1937 and 1976.

More dramatic if only because it's more recent, however, is the site of the 1991 collapse. From the parking area, look across the lake and to the left to see where an eighty-foot-long section of bank slipped down, leaving a forty-five-degree slope only a few feet from water's edge.

If you're lucky, a loon will serenade you as you watch. If you're inclined, take a picnic lunch in the campground. And if the traffic is light, as you sit on the high banks overlooking the water, you can easily mistake this place for wilderness.

How to get there: On M-33 about ten miles south of Onaway (in Presque Isle County), turn east onto Tomahawk Lake Highway. Follow this gravel road for 2.2 miles until you see the sign indicating to turn left down the dirt road to the sinkholes and Shoepac Lake. Less than a mile down the dirt road, just beyond the entrance to the Shoepac Lake Campground, you'll see a parking area at the lake on the left. The sinkholes pathway begins near the top of the rise on the right.

ISLAND PARK

This small park is surprising in that it offers features not usually found in city limits: wildlife viewing, an assortment of natural settings in a small area, and the opportunity to make a quick escape from the crowds and the noise of the city.

Before you walk across to the island, you'll probably want to take time out to watch the ducks and geese that gather in the Alpena Wildlife Sanctuary along the banks of the Thunder Bay River. Actually, the entire sanctuary encompasses 500 acres of nearby wetlands. The park is easy for people to get to and has become a favorite spot for feeding the birds and watching their youngsters grow during the summer months. Bird species common to the area include mallard ducks, Canada geese, mute swans, terns, great blue herons, and several species of songbirds.

At seventeen acres in area, Island Park is just about a mile in circumference, and several trails meander around and across it. Following the trails, you'll encounter an intriguing variety of plant species, for the area is in various stages of succession. Close to the shore you'll see marshy areas. And in the lowlands, cedar predominates. On higher ground, you'll find hardwoods. At the crest of the hill are grassy fields. On the southwest corner of the island is a beach grass planting to protect the fragile dune area. At four spots along the shoreline trails, fishing/viewing platforms await interested hikers.

For years, this area was known as "Sportsmen's Island" because it was owned and watched over by the Alpena Sportsmen's Club. It was dedicated as a memorial to the fighting forces of World War II. The main, barked trail leads uphill to a flagpole near to which white pines were planted in memory of those who gave their lives during the war.

Strange, after all those years, that the pines remain so small, still dwarfed by the memories of many of the visitors. But by the next generation or so, the link of living memory will have dissolved, leaving only the pines as a testimony to the war dead.

Near the flagpole is a deck that gives a sweeping view of the Thunder Bay River and several other small islands in the area. Actually, the deck overlooks most of the Blue Heron Canoe Water Trail, which offers canoeists an hour's glide through several points of interest.

The island is open to foot traffic. A locked gate with a passage for pedestrians prevents an onslaught of motorized vehicles. Those requiring walking aids can request a key to the gate from the front desk of the Holiday Inn across the street. Be insistent; seasonal workers aren't always aware of the key. While the main path and viewing deck were intended to be handicapped accessible, wheelchair users would need a strong assistant to help push them up the path.

How to get there: On US 23 North through the city of Alpena (in Alpena County), the first traffic light north of the bridge is at Long Rapids Road. Turn west onto Long Rapids, then left into the roadside park. At the end of the parking lot closest to US 23 is the walkway to Island Park.

General information: For a brochure outlining highlights of the Blue Heron Canoe Water Trail or for more details about Island Park, contact the Alpena Volunteer Center, Alpena Community College, 666 Johnson Street, Alpena, MI 49707-1495; 517-356-9021.

HARTWICK PINES STATE PARK

A unique setting, proximity to other attractions, a modern campground, and the ease with which it can be reached from downstate—these elements make Hartwick Pines State Park an attraction that can easily become an overnight destination.

The Michigan Forest Visitor Center at Hartwick is the newest feature included in this book. Opened in the spring of 1994, the center, a log structure itself, offers a glimpse of the importance of forestry, lumbering, and forest products to the state's history, economy, and ecology. Through massive windows, the center tantalizes visitors with a view of the forest wherein lurk forty-nine acres of virgin pines.

Inside the center, be sure to take time to watch the fourteen-minute slide presentation "The Forest: Michigan's Renewable Resource," which teaches that Michigan's forests are among the world's youngest, taking root only after the Ice Age. Another exhibit uses computer simulations to explain what foresters do and what "forest management" means. You'll get an idea of the life and death of forests as well as the effects of climate, soil, and land formations on their development. The "Nature's City" inter-active display lets you match the sounds of the forests with mounted specimens of the animals that make them. And careful! "Don't Touch the Wolf," the sign says, beneath the mounted wolf. Instead, pet the piece of wolf pelt in the wolf-shaped cut-out to get a surprise.

From the visitors center, you can take a leisurely stroll along the Virgin Pines Foot Trail. For the most part, the trail is black-topped and handicapped accessible. Be sure to pick up a free pamphlet that guides you to the numbered features along the trail. Although the trail is not quite a mile long, allow at least an hour to acquaint yourself with its features.

After a couple of minutes of walking through the maple, beech, and hemlock climax forest, you'll come to the logging camp. There, you'll see the "big wheels" that were used to move logs over hard ground and the log jammer that was used to load them onto sleds. The camp was built by the Civilian Conservation Corps in 1935 as a tribute to the loggers who had worked the area during the "White Pine Era," 1840 to 1910. To put things into perspective, consider the fact that the dollar value of the timber cut in Michigan was greater than that of all the gold mined in California during the same period. The sawmill in the camp is operated on special weekends during the summer.

Farther along, you'll reach one of the state's last remaining stands of virgin pines, some 300 to 500 years old, but it's not a dark grove of pine trees only. Where storms and age have dropped pine trees, other tree species that are intolerant of shade have cropped up. And here and there shafts of sunlight pierce through to the ground, enough so that instead of a forest floor consisting of a carpet of pine needles, ground cover flourishes. Quiet and serene, the setting is often punctuated by the incongruous thunder of big guns in the distance, for the nearby town of Grayling is home to a National Guard training camp.

The Monarch Pine is the big feature of the pine stand. It once stood 155 feet tall, but in 1992, high winds gave it a haircut, taking about thirty to forty feet off the top. It remains, however, an impressive sight.

The Mertz Grade Foot Trail shares a tangent with the Virgin Pines Trail. The Mertz Grade actually crosses M-93 and is about a two-mile loop that takes at least an hour to cover. It traverses other spots of varying topography and dominant plants as it circles Hartwick Lake.

Other trails, not as well developed, line this state park, enough so that it becomes a favorite locale for mountain biking, cross-country skiing, and snowmobiling. During hunting seasons, state park property outside the virgin forest and developed areas is open to hunting. Except for wheelchairs, no wheeled vehicles are allowed on the foot trails.

How to get there: Just north of Grayling (in Crawford County), from I-75, take exit 259 to M-93. Turn right and continue for about two miles to the park entrance on the left.

General information: A motor vehicle permit is required for entry into Hartwick Pines State Park and the Michigan Forest Visitor Center. For brochures, current hours of operation, and upcoming special events, contact Hartwick Pines State Park, Route 3, Box 3840, Grayling, MI 49738; 517-348-7068.

AU SABLE RIVER CANOE FLOAT

As a state-designated Natural River, the Au Sable is saturated with canoeists and inner-tubers during the peak summer season.

But if you like odds that favor your encountering more bald eagles than other canoeists, try a late winter float.

The allure of this stretch of the river—aside from the moderately easy paddling it entails—is the fact that it flows through the Mason Tract, land that was conveyed to the state by the late George W. Mason in 1955. One condition under which the land was conveyed was that the property "will be kept in its natural state."

So a float through the Mason Tract will get you to the heart of land that has been allowed to revert to as natural a state as it can, considering that the Au Sable at one time was a major highway for loggers. The log rollway at the High Banks is evidence of their work. That is just downstream of Durant's Castle, the flagstone basement of which is all that remains.

A drift through the Mason Tract is not complete without a stop at The Chapel, built in Mason's memory, a reminder to all of us that we are enjoying a gift from a man who considered his time on the river to be a gift itself.

And if the river gods indulge your dreams, you may find that you will likewise be blessed with many chance encounters with nature. Consider our running list of species viewed and special treats as you read some notes from our own trips:

"Over three hundred turkeys. An otter. Three eagle sightings. Four grouse. A mink. Goshawk, plus, once again, another hawk we couldn't positively I.D. Pileated woodpecker, and zillions of ducks. Especially goldeneyes and mergansers. One merganser surfaced from feeding not thirty feet from us toward shore. You could see the concern on his face as John and I floated by; he couldn't back up any further, and there just was not enough water between him and the canoe for him to taxi to his takeoff. A split second after we passed, however, he was streaking across the river and lifting toward the sky.

"We also noted several black ducks and a few mallards. Lots of chickadees and more blue jays than you could count, including a flock of about seventy."

The high point for us one year actually happened twice: "We saw bald eagles feeding on their prey, one on a merganser, the other on what looked from a distance to be a raccoon."

Part of the challenge of seeing the eagles or the 300 white-tailed deer we viewed on another trip is to paddle as quietly as possible. "Saturday provided a team highlight as we were able to count the number of paddle clunks on the canoe using the digits of only one hand—with two fingers left over."

On another trip, "One of the neatest things to see was the one grouse who looked to be strutting—kind of getting ready for mating season. He had those black ruffs on his neck pumped up, as well as the cape down the back of his neck. The other heart pounder came when those seven young tom turkeys decided they wanted to get to the other side of the river and flew across, smack dab in front of us. Man, were they big—they looked like para-trooper transports crossing the English Channel for D-Day!"

Special sightings have come when we've seen deer in the exact spots where deer had been in previous years. The best of that type was a big deer that was sunning itself on the riverbank and calmly looked up and watched us drift quietly past, no more than thirty yards away. But nothing can match that cute little yearling that crossed the stream in front of us with its mother. That was quite a sight, mom bounding from the water and baby skittering out.

Though no one can guarantee you'll see scads of wildlife, you at least will not be seeing scads of people—and that's a guarantee!

How to get there: From Roscommon, enter Crawford County on M-18. Travel east for about two miles to Chase Bridge Road. Turn left onto Chase Bridge and go north for about two miles to the bridge and public access to the South Branch of the Au Sable. Arrange for pickup or have your car spotted at the Smith Bridge access, which is about twelve miles away on the north side of M-72 as it crosses the South Branch. At a leisurely pace, this

Rafts of up to a dozen hooded mergansers can be seen in the fall and winter floating in rivers, searching for small fish and amphibians

trip should take you about four hours. There are no take-outs between Chase and Smith bridges.

General information: For maps and other information, contact the DNR Region II Headquarters, 8717 North Roscommon Road, Roscommon, MI 48653; 517-275-5151.

You can also contact the Roscommon Chamber of Commerce at 517-275-8760.

KIRTLAND'S WARBLER NESTING AREAS

Inexperienced birders are advised to contact the Fish and Wildlife Service to make arrangements for tours, which run,

ROUGHING IT EASY—AND SMART

For a late winter/early spring canoe-camp trip, you might benefit from some rules we've developed, both through experimentation and exquisite hindsight.

First, realize that you are putting yourself into a survival situation. Be sure to bring two pairs of warm winter boots, waterproof if possible, along with a complete set of dry clothes. And that includes rain gear. Basically, you have be prepared for winter's worst, two times over. As with most clothing for outdoor activities, the operant words are "layering" and "comfort." Dress in layers you can shed to avoid overheating. Wear loose enough clothes so you aren't restricted in your movements. You'll be doubly glad to be wearing your life vest. Aside from the protection it will give in the event you capsize, the floatation material will also provide insulation against the cold as you paddle along.

Be sure to take along a pruning saw in case you encounter a few limbs from windfalls blocking your way. Also, take some extra lengths of rope to help you haul the canoe overland, sled-style, if your way is blocked or icy river conditions require portages.

Finally, you will be glad you've taken the extra time and effort to pack a stove for cooking a shore lunch. Just remember that instead of using a cooler to keep your food cold, in many cases you'll be using it to insulate the food from freezing temperatures. You might consider storing a stew or some chili in the container in which you will be cooking it. That way, even if it does freeze, you won't have to worry about scooping it into a cooking pot. And don't forget to keep a watchful eye on your drinking water so it doesn't freeze.

typically, from May 15 through July 4. To accommodate late-nesting birds, the areas usually stay closed to the public until August 15. Contrary to popular belief, however, it's not illegal to drive the county roads through the nesting areas. Anyone who knows what to listen for may legally drive the roads and listen for the song of the male Kirtland's warbler. In fact, 1994 marked the opening of the east loop of the Jack Pine Wildlife Tour. This self-guided auto tour will eventually total nearly 100 miles and will meander through several counties. Interpretive signs will be placed at several spots along the tour.

The reason the areas are closed is simple: the birds nest on the ground. In the coarse Grayling sand, a female will hollow out a depression little bigger than a tennis ball. She'll line it with leaves, twigs, and blades of the plants and grasses that grow in the area. Such a lining also provides camouflage, and walking through the areas, you could crush the precious contents of a nest without even realizing it.

Why all the attention and concern given to a bird that is little bigger than a goldfinch, and though a little more full in the body, about the same size as a house sparrow? That's simple. The Kirtland's warbler is an endangered species. Northern Michigan is the only nesting area in the world for these little birds.

Biologists figure that Michigan's appeal lies in its combination of jack pine stands with the aforementioned Grayling soil. The warblers are very particular about their choice of nesting habitats, and it's jack pine stands. Jack pines appear in other areas of the United States and Canada but not in the same soil. Consequently, they are devoid of breeding pairs. Jack pines are just about the only tree that thrives in the Grayling sand, and the ground cover of blueberry, sweet fern, sand cherry, lichen, and several types of sedges and grasses suits the needs of the birds for nest construction.

So particular are the birds that not just any such jack pine stand will do. For their nesting requirements, they prefer pine stands from about eight to twenty years in age. Trees in that age class run from about five to fifteen feet tall. Much taller than that and they begin to space out, allowing more light to hit the ground, which changes the ground cover's composition. Plus they offer more hiding spots from which sharp-shinned hawks can hunt the warblers. So, when we say "northern Michigan jack pine stands" here, we're not talking about the towering, swaying pines often portrayed as the memory of Michigan's once virgin forests.

Singing male Kirtland's warblers have actually been located in eight counties of northern Michigan, and the various lands on which they've been found are administered by the U.S. Forest Service, Fish and Wildlife Service, or the DNR. To meet the nesting requirements of the tiny visitors which winter in the Bahamas, the habitat is being managed according to a Recovery Plan developed in 1976. As might be expected, to keep the habitat prime, the various agencies must get rid of the trees that are no longer of interest to the warblers. They do this usually in a combination of two basic ways: commercial timber harvesting and "prescribed fires."

Probably the most famous of these fires prescribed for habitat management is the only one that has ever gotten out of control, the Mack Lake Fire of May 5, 1980, which quickly became an overdose instead of a prescription. The scar from the fire can still be seen where it jumped M-33 about five miles south of Mio and where, coincidentally, the Jack Pine Wildlife Tour begins. One Forest Service employee was killed in the fire, and over forty dwellings were destroyed as the fire smothered over 25,000 acres. The irony that is nature, however, now dictates that about 60 percent of the warbler population has been counted in the 7,000 to 10,000 acres of warbler habitat that developed as a result of the fire.

The Forest Service and DNR have established other programs of planting pine seedlings in areas that have been previously cleared through commercial harvest. On a hot summer day, it's easy to understand why such areas are called "barrens." It's difficult to imagine these upland deserts appealing to anything except the scrawny jack pines and seemingly parched ground cover. Here and there among the pines, burned-out trees rise as tall as they can, like solitary old men trying to retain their dignity in a park full of youngsters. These "snags" are left standing as an attractant to both the male Kirtland's warbler and Eastern bluebirds, which like to use them as perches.

If you take a guided tour, you are just about guaranteed that

**Kirtland warblers summer in Michigan beneath the jack pines
and winter in Bermuda**

you will hear a bird sing, and there's a very good chance that
you'll see one. You are encouraged to bring spotting scopes and
binoculars. Plus, you're welcome to take photographs from the
road.

Don't plan on bringing along a tape recorder, for they are
forbidden. The problem is, if you tape a singing male, then play
it back to another singing male, you will put unnecessary stress
on the second bird. He will react in an aggressive way, kind of
like the way a parakeet reacts when he thinks he sees another bird
staring at him from a mirror in his cage.

Groups of fewer than four don't need reservations. But the agencies running the tours maintain different schedules. If you are in the area and get the urge to hear a bird sing, pay attention to the weather forecasts. The male warblers aren't as active in excessive heat, cold, heavy rain, or high winds. In other words, the days that would be most comfortable for you to listen are the days the birds would be most likely to sing.

How to get there: The U.S. Fish and Wildlife Service offers free guided tours out of Grayling (in Crawford County), and the U.S. Forest Service runs tours out of Mio (in Oscoda County). Grayling is located at exit 254 of I-75. You can reach Mio via M-33, about thirty-five miles north of exit 202 of I-75.

General information: To find out about tours to Kirtland's warbler nesting areas, contact the U.S. Fish and Wildlife Service, East Lansing Field Office, 1405 South Harrison Road, East Lansing, MI 48823; 517-337-6650 (Grayling tours); or the U.S. Forest Service District Ranger, Huron National Forest, Mio, MI 48647; 517-826-3252 (Mio tours).

For general information about the warblers and the management of their habitat, contact either of those offices or the DNR Wildlife Division, P.O. Box 30180, Dept. KW, Lansing, MI 48909; 517-373-9453.

The first annual Kirtland's Warbler Festival was held in 1994. For information on upcoming festivals, maps for the Jack Pine Wildlife Tour, or a county travel guide, contact the Chamber of Commerce for Oscoda County, P.O. Box 670, Mio, MI 48647; 800-800-6133 or 517-826-3331.

PIGEON RIVER COUNTRY STATE FOREST

The Pigeon River Country State Forest (PRC) offers unique opportunities in the Lower Peninsula to people who desire quiet areas, room to roam, and a chance to see some of the most special and spectacular wildlife in the state.

A massive area of 98,000 mostly contiguous acres in Otsego and Cheboygan Counties, the PRC is the only state forest whose management is overseen by an outside group, the Pigeon River Country Advisory Council. This group formed in direct response to the threat posed by oil companies when they first wanted to develop the area for drilling back in the 1970s. One of the outcomes produced by the council is a concept of management for the PRC. Number one on its list of objectives is "to provide favorable habitat for elk." Every other objective falls in, respectfully, behind.

The PRC lies in the heart of Michigan's elk country, home of the largest herd east of the Mississippi. Descendants of the seven that were planted here in 1918, the elk now number about 1,300 and are the big draw to the PRC. In fact, two spots have been "enhanced" by the state in an effort to encourage the elk to continue to congregate there. These "elk viewing areas" are clearly marked and are easily reached by car.

Other than those two areas, however, and with the exception of some of the campgrounds, lakes and ponds, and parts of three rivers, most places cannot be reached by car. In an effort to maintain the wild character of the PRC, to protect the land from overuse, and to provide animals with insulation from too much human intrusion, many, many trails have been closed to motorized vehicles. Additionally, the forest contains over sixty miles of pathways, including two-thirds of the seventy-mile High Country Pathway and the entire twelve miles of the Shingle Mill Pathway spur. These design features encourage people to travel to places on foot, to be quiet, and to try to experience the PRC as a wild place where they but temporarily belong.

The PRC can easily become an overnight destination for those willing to camp under rustic conditions and take the necessary time simply to wander around. Dozens and dozens of trails to no place special let you discover special places of and on your own, to escape the mechanized world, to focus on wildflowers, berries, or morels (wild mushrooms, in spring), or to attempt to spot other wildlife.

Besides the elk, other animals, such as white-tailed deer, wild turkeys, and black bears, range through the PRC. Also, though more difficult to view, bobcats and pine martens roam the wild country. Near the ponds and lakes, be on the lookout for loons, ospreys, and bald eagles, especially at the Dog Lake Wild Area.

Dog Lake, along with the Pine Natural Area and the Grindstone Creek Hardwoods Natural Area, shows the diversity of the topography of the PRC. Lowlands and wetlands, pine stands, hardwoods – the PRC has them all. The three river courses add high hills and valleys to the terrain. In fact, the PRC's foresters claim that nowhere else in the Lower Peninsula can you find such diversity of desirable "wild" characteristics in such magnitude as you can find in the PRC.

Getting Around

Taking a drive through the PRC accomplishes little more than adding miles to your car's odometer. You might catch a glimpse of an elk, but you won't begin to touch the spirit of Pigeon River Country. You need to get out of your car.

If you decide to hike, you should have little problem if you stay on marked hiking or bridle trails. As ever, though, once you leave the paved roads and your vehicle, you should always carry a map and a compass.

Even PRC foresters admit that the hundreds of logging trails lacing the area are difficult to map accurately. Under these conditions, the best pieces of advice are (1) no matter what map you use, trust it only for the major trails and roads and (2) realize that most of the time you will be no more than a mile from a county road.

Listen for the bull elk calling at Pigeon River in the fall

During winter, paved roads in the PRC are plowed. Other than that, nothing else in the forest is maintained. This means that skiers, snowshoers, or winter campers must begin their treks from county roads and carry in all their gear. It also means that trails will not be groomed. A good place to set up a winter camp or to begin a day's ski trip is at Pigeon Bridge Forest Campground, about two-thirds of the way along Sturgeon Valley Road between Vanderbilt and the PRC headquarters. This is also the start of the Shingle Mill Pathway. From here, skiers have their choices among the shorter, easier loops on the pathway, or the longer ones, which provide the best views but are also the most difficult to ski. Those looking for a longer ski trip can also join the High Country Pathway from the campground.

How to get there: From I-75, take exit 290 to the town of Vanderbilt (in Otsego County). In town, turn east (left) at the blinking light and head down Main Street. The name later changes to Sturgeon Valley Road, and the blacktop changes to gravel. About 13.5 miles from town, you'll come to the log cabin headquarters of the Pigeon River Country State Forest.

General information: If you drive to the PRC headquarters, don't expect a DNR interpreter to be available to answer all your questions. Unlike state parks, the state forests have no budget for such jobs. You'll find a load of information on the history and development of the area, its features and highlights. In fact, your tour should begin with at least a half-hour stop at the headquarters so you can read the history and get a feel for the Pigeon River Country.

Area maps, Elk Tour maps, and maps to campgrounds and other attractions are available at the forest headquarters or by mail. For a prompt response, send a stamped, self-addressed envelope to Pigeon River Country State Forest, 9966 Twin Lakes Road, Vanderbilt, MI 49795; 517-983-4101.

WILDLIFE VIEWING STRATEGIES

Viewing wildlife in the Pigeon River Country State Forest—or anywhere else in Michigan, for that matter—is rarely a case of driving to an *X* someone has drawn for you on a map.

For example, the Elk Tour map from the PRC headquarters indicates several spots west of highway M-33 where you should expect to see elk. Yet I've seen as many elk on the east side, especially along Voyer Lake Road, which is about a quarter mile north of the DNR Field Office in Atlanta. Voyer Lake Road at M-33 is the beginning of a fifty-mile drive through the Mackinaw State Forest, and it takes about a twelve-mile meander on graded, dirt roads until it hits blacktopped County Road 624, which can be taken back to the west to return to M-33.

Should you drive out—no matter on which side of M-33—remember that spring and fall are the best time to see the elk, especially in open fields at daybreak and dusk.

The elk do not concentrate in summer and can be anywhere. Since summer heat is unpredictable, you've probably got a better chance of seeing elk if you take an early morning drive. But be in the woods by daylight, for as soon as the sun starts to heat things up, the elk start to head to the cool, shady pine plantations deep within the forest.

From mid-September to late October, keep an ear out to hear an elk "bugle." This call is the bull elk's method of asserting his dominance in his territory and of attracting the cows that will make up his harem for the upcoming breeding season. This is the time when the elk are the most active.

In winter, look for the elk near recently cut stands of timber. They will feed on the sprouts and any cuttings they can get to.

In fact, winter is a great time to strap on the cross-country skis or snowshoes, head out for the Pigeon River Country or any secluded area, and look for other animals, too. Not just the animals themselves, you see, but also the stories they leave in their tracks. For example, during the brutally cold, snow-laden winter of 1994, the only place we saw any elk was along the longest loop of the Shingle Mill Pathway as far from cars and other people as we could get. We wouldn't have known to be alert for them had we not recognized their tracks: they had been using the foot trail as their most convenient highway.

Finally, the town of Atlanta bills itself as the "Elk Capital" of Michigan. Driving through town, notice the mounted elk displayed in front of the post office. Nearby an interpretive plaque placed by the Michigan Outdoor Writers Association gives a history of the elk herd in Michigan.

For additional information on possible elk viewing hot spots, try contacting the Atlanta Chamber of Commerce, P.O. Box 410, Atlanta, MI 49709.

A novel way to move through the PRC is on horseback. You'll be away from most other people, it's a different way to experience the area, and on horseback humans are usually able to get a closer view of the elk. Contact Vern Bishop in nearby Onaway after 11 P.M.; 517-733-6463.

THE GRASS FARM

The Grass Farm is the name of a summer attraction, in Montmorency County, that offers people the opportunity to view white-tailed deer and wild turkeys from the comfort of their vehicles.

In the box above, I said that viewing wildlife in Michigan rarely is as simple as heading for an *X* someone's made on a map for you. Well, the Grass Farm is one of the rarities, and I'm making the *X*. From late afternoon to dark on any summer evening, look for dozens, perhaps more than a hundred, white-tailed deer feeding in these open areas. Quite often they are joined by wild turkeys in smaller numbers. Look on both sides of the road all the way up to M-32.

This is not a secret spot; you'll be joined by several others, tourists and locals alike, who realize that seeing wildlife on this loop is almost a 100 percent guaranteed proposition. Wildlife doesn't get much more predictable than this.

The deer are used to the parade of vehicles, and remain at ease as long as people remain inside. This allows you to view a more natural behavior as opposed to watching animals on guard. You may see a couple of young bucks in a mock sparring match or, later in the summer, a solitary deer on its hind legs reverse-bobbing for apples that are still hanging in the trees.

The land in the area is private, all the more reason to remain in your vehicle.

How to get there: From the town of Atlanta, take M-32/33 east about six miles to the split, then follow M-33 south for about three miles to Carter Road (County 451 on pre-1995 maps). Take Carter east for three miles, then turn south onto Klein, the dirt road. Follow this road for two miles until it turns east and becomes Weber Creek Road. Continue for almost another two miles until you reach Farrier Road. Turn north onto Farrier. The fields begin on the left.

General information: For a county map, write the Montmorency County Road Commission, Route 2, Box 625, Atlanta, MI 49709. The Grass Farm is located in section 10 of Rust Township.

4

Northwest

SLEEPING BEAR DUNES NATIONAL LAKESHORE

Although the myth of the Sleeping Bear includes a couple of
slight variations in interpretation, the reality has only one: the
mound of sand that the Ojibwa once used as a landmark is disap-
pearing. Waves pound and erode the base of the plateau on which
the dune rests, and then some more sand collapses onto the
beach. Wind helps blow sand away and destroys plant cover that
would otherwise provide relative stability to the dune. Old photographs in the interpretive area of the visitors center show how the
dune is losing its personality. Where it once stood over 230 feet
high, by 1980 it had melted to only 103 feet. So if you want to see
the Sleeping Bear, you need to hurry, and you need to use your
imagination to try to envision what the Indians saw.

And what the Ojibwa saw is the basis of the myth, which
goes like this: a bear and her two cubs set out from Wisconsin to
swim across Lake Michigan. The cubs tired and drowned. The
mother got to shore, curled up, and went to sleep, forever awaiting her doomed children. Now, here's where the myths vary:

North and South Manitou Islands, about twenty miles out in Lake Michigan, either are the cubs or were raised by the Great Spirit to mark the spot where the cubs died. Likewise, the dune either is the bear or was created to mark the spot where she awaited.

You have to be careful with terms around here, for "Sleeping Bear" applies to several important points of concern: the entire National Lakeshore, the single dune, or the general area of dunes wherein lies the specific dune. The Sleeping Bear Dunes area covers about four square miles of the National Lakeshore's total of 106 square miles in Leelanau and Benzie Counties, M-109 passes between the east side of the Sleeping Bear Dunes and Little Glen Lake. Here's where you'll find the one spot where people are encouraged to climb the dunes. That's why it's understandable that visitors might focus on this small spot and ignore the other 102 square miles.

The Sleeping Bear dune, with the sand piled atop a plateau, is called a *perched* dune. The other type of dune, more common, is called a *beach* dune, which as the name indicates, is a much smaller mound, comprised mostly of beach sand on low-lying areas along a shore. Both types can be found in the park.

Don't miss the slide show at this visitors center. One highlight gives you an idea of how a park famous for its miles of elevated beach, for crying out loud, can be enjoyed in winter. More impressive are the spectacular aerial views that provide a

---

NOT A QUICK STOP

If you plan to use this park merely as a stopping point, be forewarned: once you rush to the top at the dune climb, you still face about a 3.5-mile round-trip walk to the cliff overlooking Lake Michigan. So, you can't simply figure on rushing up the dune, rushing down, dipping your toes in the water, rushing up, rolling down, and heading out for some shopping.

---

wonderful perspective, a literal "overview" of the dunes and lakeshore.

Once you see things from that perspective, you'll want to get to know the National Lakeshore on terms more intimate than just your running up a hill and leaving. And there are plenty of terms to consider.

A dozen trails are located throughout the park, and surprisingly, not all of them traipse over hills of sand. Some cover beech-maple forests and even pine plantations and stands of other mixed evergreens. About fifty-five miles of trails let you get away on foot, on skis, or on snowshoes. Their terrains range from flat to gently rolling, to hilly, to steep and rugged. As in all places that are open to the public, autumn hikers here are reminded to wear fluorescent orange clothing during hunting seasons (September to January). Bicycles are prohibited on hiking trails.

Relatively short and pleasant canoe trips are available on the Platte River in the southern part of the park and the Crystal River in the north.

If you prefer to reach a few panoramas without leaving the road, try driving or biking the Pierce Stocking Scenic Drive, a 7.4-mile loop that allows you to view things from the top of the Sleeping Bear Dunes area. It includes stops for a hike atop a dune and one for a view of the Sleeping Bear. Interpretive pamphlets are available at the visitors center or at the beginning of the loop, off M-109.

Campers will find a variety of possibilities, both within the park and nearby. Accommodations range from primitive, walk-in campsites to private campgrounds, and everything in between.

Guided walks and evening programs are held throughout the summer.

How to get there: In Leelanau/Benzie Counties, take M-72 west out of Traverse City for twenty-two miles to its western terminus, where you'll see the Sleeping Bear Visitor Center on the north side of the road before you get to downtown Empire.

General information: The Park Service is well prepared to offer in-depth information about the park, its hiking trails, the geology of the dunes, and the Maritime Museum at the Sleeping Bear Point Coast Guard Station. Be sure to request the pamphlet "Plant Life," which gives a nice explanation about the various zones of plants from the shore inland. The visitors center is open from 9:00 A.M. to 6:00 P.M. every day except Thanksgiving and Christmas.

Contact the Superintendent, Sleeping Bear Dunes National Lakeshore, P.O. Box 277, Empire, MI 49630; 616-326-5134.

JORDAN RIVER PATHWAY

You can make this trip a simple day hike or a two-day backpacking excursion through one of the most picturesque valleys you'll find in the state, that of the Jordan River, dedicated in 1972 as Michigan's first Natural Scenic River.

Our most memorable visit to this area in Antrim County was several years ago, parking where the snowplows had stopped, strapping on the snowshoes, and hiking for half an hour to get to the beginning of our five-minute walk to the top of Deadman's Hill.

This jewel of a lookout invites with personalities that change with the seasons. Winter is the extrovert, offering the best view of the Jordan River as it flows from its headwaters along Old State Road to the north through the valley below. Spring teases with promise. Summer teems with luxurious growth. And fall, in all its vibrant glory, must simply be nature's version of Dylan Thomas's reminder "Do not go gentle into that good night."

The pathway begins here. Its two loops are three and eighteen miles each, with a few segments crossing county roads, so you can customize your hike. You'll walk the gamut, from upland hardwoods and mixed conifers to lowland swamp areas. Be on the lookout for white-tailed deer and red fox. A side hike to O'Brien Pond north of the pathway may reward you with a view of a great egret.

Even if you don't hike the trails, be sure to take time to drive part of Old State Road below, just to become aware of things you can't notice from the hill.

How to get there: In Antrim County, from Gaylord, travel west on M-32 for eleven miles to US 131. Turn south on 131 for 1.5 miles and turn west onto Deadman's Hill Road. Follow this dirt road for two miles to the parking spot. It's a five-minute walk to the top of the hill.

General information: For an interpretive map of the pathway, write to the Fire and Recreation Specialist, Mackinaw State Forest District, DNR, Box 667, Gaylord, MI 49735; 517-732-3541.

GRASS RIVER NATURAL AREA (GRNA)

A place for quiet walks and educational programs, the GRNA is surprisingly pristine, given its proximity to some of the heavily visited tourist areas in the state. This place is a microcosm. It has to be, for the river it borders is only 2.5 miles long. As part of Antrim County's "Chain of Lakes," the Grass River links Lake Bellaire to Clam Lake. Owned by the county and administered by a nonprofit corporation of volunteers, this natural area encompasses 1,100 acres, only 225 of which are generally open to the public.

But don't let the size fool you. The small space includes a wide variety of habitat types. From the parking lot, take the Cabin Trail to the interpretive center and river trailheads. On your way, you'll pass through mixed hardwoods, which give way to lowland conifers. Much of the Sedge Meadow Trail to the river consists of a boardwalk over the marsh, so visitors can see what the marsh is like without disturbing it. Also found in the

**Thick winter fur and a wraparound tail insulate red foxes
even in the coldest weather**

area are other upland and marsh forests, meadows, wetlands, a creek, and of course the river.

Living here, according to environmental surveys, are over 400 species of plants, 49 species of mammals, and 65 species of birds. Tucked away, half a mile in from a secondary road, the GRNA is the type of place where you'd expect to see deer early in the morning should you sneak in for a visit. The GRNA is open year-round from dawn to dusk. Things are so quiet and calm back there that it just seems right that deer would show up. Besides, something has to be responsible for all the deer tracks punctuating the road.

This is a good spot for hiking and nature photography, "passive recreational opportunities," the GRNA board says. No bikes are allowed on trails. As in all natural areas, you'll be asked to leave plants and flowers alone. A most interesting regulation can be inferred from the lack of picnic tables within the GRNA. As its brochure explains, "We feel that there are more suitable areas elsewhere for picnicking." Also, naturalists are usually available on-site during daylight hours.

The group has completed its land acquisitions. More and more effort will now be directed toward education. If you are planning to come to this part of the state, be sure to write for a copy of the programs being held during the time of your visit. You'll probably want to plan a day around some of the workshops that are held for kids and families. For example: "Celebrate eARTh," which included a singer, a poet, and a wildlife artist; "Conscientious Camping" which trains participants in the techniques of minimum-impact camping; "Loon Life"; and "Wild Flower Wakenings." The group has recently begun offering winter workshops, too.

Because it's publicly owned, because it's cared for by volunteers, because it offers families a special place to learn along with others or on their own, because of the spirit that infuses its existence, the Grass River Natural Area is the kind of place I'd hoped to find while researching this book.

How to get there: From Bellaire (in Antrim County), head south on M-88 about four miles until you are faced with taking a decisive left turn in order to stay on the highway. Instead of turning, go straight onto Comfort Road. Follow Comfort for two miles until you reach Alden Road. Turn right onto Alden and look for the entrance to the GRNA half a mile down the road, on the right side. Coming from Mancelona, just go straight on Alden Highway when you have to choose between that and bearing to the right on M-88 to Bellaire. A limited amount of docking space is also available for those arriving by boat.

General information: For a map and sample newsletter, write to the Grass River Natural Area, Inc., P.O. Box 231, Bellaire, MI 49615; 616-533-8314.

SOUTH MANITOU ISLAND

Of the three northwestern Michigan islands generally available to tourists, the 5,260-acre South Manitou is like Baby Bear, offering a nature-loving Goldilocks an experience that is "just right." Conveniently enough, according to another tale, the Ojibwa Indian myth, South Manitou along with its sister island, North Manitou, represents the spot where two bear cubs died on their way across Lake Michigan from Wisconsin. The Sleeping Bear Dune on the mainland is their mother.

South Manitou is "just right" because it offers a taste of wilderness without satiating. People wanting to escape the tumult of the crowds in what should be the sleepy fishing port of Leland can get themselves to the island and enjoy a picnic on the beach without expending much energy. Those seeking a wilderness hike can set out to cover as much territory as they are up to during the tour boat's four-hour layover at the dock. Neophyte backpackers can enjoy an exotic overnight stay while not testing themselves too much: the campground farthest from the dock is only 3.7 miles away, and the island by shoreline is only ten miles around. Camping is allowed only at the three designated areas.

If you hike, you might consider the perched sand dunes on the western side of the island as your farthest point of travel on a day trip. But don't be misled by the information on the map you'll find on the brochure. The round-trip to the sand dunes may only be 7.4 miles. But if you want to climb them and see the lake, you can expect to traverse about another 1.5 miles of back dunes and sand valleys before you gaze at the clear waters of Lake Michigan, about 450 feet below.

The view is worth it, though. When I visited, the water was so clear that from the top of the dune I watched a fish swimming near shore. I even snapped a photo but have trouble convincing anyone that the dark spot in the middle of my picture is anything more than—well, a dark spot that somehow got in the middle of the picture.

Another treat you'll enjoy is relative solitude as you perch atop a perched dune. Unlike the dune climb on the mainland portion of the National Lakeshore, these hills are not visited by hundreds of people a day. Also, most day visitors seem to fall off along the way or to take some of the guided tours in motorized vehicles, so if you're up to it, you should be king—or queen—of the sand hill for the time being.

One note of caution, however: if you decide to roll down a dune and follow the shore back to the dock, you will have a little longer hike back than you did out to the dunes, and with no marked paths. Depending on the effects of waves and the water levels, you might have to do a lot of hiking in water up to your knees.

At any rate, either on your outbound or return hike, be sure to stop off to see the wreck of the *Francisco Morazan*, an Italian freighter that sank in November 1960. You'll also want to step into the Valley of the Giant Cedars, 500-year-old trees that lord it over visitors and other trees alike. The cedars were spared the effects of logging because they grow in an area that was just too inaccessible for loggers in the nineteenth century.

The side trails to these two spots are well marked. You won't want to stop too long at either of them, however, especially during July and August. I told you that nothing gets satiated here, and that goes triple for the mosquitoes.

One reason I was able to hike so quickly to the dunes and back is that the mosquito convoy encourages the hiker to move along. No kidding. I know I looked like a goof during the lake crossing, wearing my long-sleeved shirt, long pants, and heavy socks on a beautiful, sun-drenched day. But at least on the trail I had to worry about bugs only on my face, neck, and hands while those wearing shorts and T-shirts were assaulted from tip to toe wherever a patch of skin dared appear. No kidding. The blasted bugs even bit the fleshy part of my palms, and one tried to dig in on my fingernail. I felt pretty good about my personal record toward population reduction, five with one swipe of my hand, until one lady on the return trip told me she had excised thirteen in one manual assault.

The excess of mosquitoes is easily explained. Uninitiated hikers might think that they will be trekking along sandy

---

BUG OFF!

Forget about Off and Avon Skin So Soft as effective mosquito repellents on South Manitou. They have proven to be of little help. About the only thing that does work on these bugs is Cutters. This is what the people who work on the island recommend—after you arrive on the island, of course. Travel writers who forget both the Off and the emergency supply of Skin So Soft in their cars, however, can only speculate as to the relative relief any bug repellent might have been able to afford.

---

beaches, dunes, and lakeside paths. This is true for only part of the trail system on South Manitou. Most of the time, however, the trails roam inland, through woods and lowland areas, places far from the comforting lake breezes. Be sure to protect yourself against the insects.

Better yet, plan to arrive sometime from mid-May to early June. The bugs shouldn't bother you. There will be a little less lush vegetation to obscure your view of the cedars. And the trilliums should be in full bloom, a nice, delicate, ground-level complement to the massive cedars looming above.

Other attractions for visitors to the island include Gull Point, a breeding habitat for gulls, and the South Manitou lighthouse, which acted as a beacon for ships entering the Manitou Passage between the island and the mainland. Remnants of a farmstead, a schoolhouse, and a small cemetery dot the center of the island and are easily reached from main trails.

The old U.S. Coast Guard Life Saving Station is now the Ranger Station. Day-trippers to the island should be sure to pack all their needs—including food—for there are no stores or food concessions on the island. Drinking water is available at four separate locations. Pets are not allowed.

How to get there: South Manitou Island, about sixteen miles into Lake Michigan from the town of Leland (in Leelanau County), is part of the Sleeping Bear Dunes National Lakeshore. A private concession runs day trips out of Leland. Individual boaters will find no docking or fuel services available and will have to moor their boats in the harbor.

General information: For a brochure that includes a map of South Manitou plus tour boat information, contact the Superintendent, Sleeping Bear Dunes National Lakeshore, P.O. Box 277, Empire, MI 49630; 616-326-5134.

OTHER LAKE MICHIGAN ISLANDS

In our little story, if not in the Indian myths, two other spots in the area take the roles of Papa and Mama Bear, North Manitou and Beaver Islands.

North Manitou Island, three miles from South Manitou, is the second of the two drowned bear cubs in the Ojibwa myth. But in our tale, North Manitou is Papa Bear.

At 15,000 acres, North is nearly three times larger than South. Managed as a wilderness by the Park Service, it offers features that the casual tourist might find to be "too hard." On the other hand, backpackers who desire something more challenging than South Manitou will want to give North a try. It's an overnight destination if you plan to arrive by the concession boat out of Leland, for the boat leaves immediately with no layover. Thus, you have to plan to stay at least one night.

As on South, private boaters must anchor their craft offshore. North, however, does not have a protected anchorage. You may tie up to the dock only for loading and unloading your gear.

Except for the eight campsites in the village campground, wilderness camping regulations are in effect, thus allowing you to camp wherever you want, within certain guidelines. The only spot to pick up potable drinking water is at the Ranger Station. Hiking here is more rigorous than on South, for the trails aren't always marked as well, and the terrain gets more technical.

North Manitou was under private ownership until 1984. Previous owners imported nine white-tailed deer to the island in 1926. A combination of artificial winter feeding programs and a lack of predators allowed the population to soar to an unhealthy 2,000. Since 1985, deer hunts have been held to maintain the herd at a population the island can better accommodate. You should be sure to wear fluorescent orange if you take to the trails in the fall.

Farther north, Beaver Island, in Charlevoix County, becomes Mama Bear in our tale, not because it should be rejected, like Mama Bear's bed, as being "too soft," but because of the three islands, it is the one that—historically and currently—most heavily has felt the imprint of man's footsteps.

Beaver Island remains a popular summer tourist destination as much for its human history as for its natural appeal. The island is noted as the site of the only monarchy ever established in the United States as well as being a settlement for Irish immigrants in the early 1800s.

As far as getting around goes, the Chamber of Commerce recommends you bring along some kind of vehicle on the ferry or that you rent a car or moped on the island, whose fifty-three-square-mile area makes it the largest in Lake Michigan. For a fee, bicycles can be transported on the ferry, though the Chamber recommends their use only in the village of St. James or on the five miles of paved road down the center of the Island. See what I mean about this being the "Mama Bear" of the islands if your aim is to get away from people and cars and stuff?

In the high season, you can arrange to fly to Beaver Island, and the ferry concession runs several round-trips a day from Charlevoix to the island. But the thirty-two-mile trip from Charlevoix takes about two and a half hours, so you will probably want to make Beaver Island an overnight destination. A twenty-six-slip municipal yacht dock is available for people who arrive on their own boats. Whatever method of transport you choose to get there, you should make reservations beforehand.

Little less than half the island remains a part of the Mackinaw State Forest, available for your prowls. About seven miles south of St. James, you'll find the Beaver Island State Forest Campground. Other than that, you'll have to make arrangements for a motel or cabin.

Make no mistake: Beaver Island is a jewel, certainly worth exploring. But the best presentation of the dichotomy facing visitors whose primary concern is natural appeal comes from the Chamber of Commerce itself: "Each year, more and more people come to enjoy and experience Beaver Island. As a result, much of what makes Beaver Island so special, the peace and quiet and the unique and abundant plant and animal species, are all in need of our special consideration . . ."

As with South Manitou, for a brochure that includes a map of North Manitou plus tour boat information, contact the Superintendent at Sleeping Bear Dunes National Lakeshore.

For information on Beaver Island and transportation to it, contact its Chamber of Commerce, P.O. Box 5, Beaver Island, MI 49782; 616-448-2505.

NORDHOUSE DUNES WILDERNESS AREA

What makes Nordhouse unique is the fact that it is the only nationally designated wilderness area in the Lower Peninsula. Although at only 3,450 acres it may not offer the size you imagine for a wilderness, it certainly evokes the *feel*.

To gain that feeling, enter the wilderness from the Nurnberg Road parking area. Realize that the dunes are the trophy that await you at the end of your hike. You will first traverse a hilly, rolling mature hardwood forest stand. These trees soon give way to lowland marsh species near Nordhouse Lake. At a casual pace, you should take more than half an hour to wend your way to the back dunes. Notice the pockets of jack pine and juniper that dot the dunes.

Once on the shore of Lake Michigan, if you are lucky, you will feel either privileged or insignificant. For if you're lucky, you'll have the place to yourself, and you'll enjoy a view of the lake, the beach, and the dunes uninterrupted by any indication of human interference. You'll be in the middle of nearly three miles of undeveloped beach overlooked by the dunes, some of which reach a height of 140 feet.

As you might expect, Michigan's western shoreline is popular for sundown viewing. The view from the shore at Nordhouse, however, is special because you have to earn it. No motorized or mechanical vehicles are allowed in designated wilderness areas. This means, especially, *no mountain bikes*. Plus, though the system contains nearly fifteen miles of trails, they aren't signed, except at the trailheads. So if you decide to hike in for a sunset experience, realize it must be a *hike*, not a ride. And realize that you'll need to pay careful attention to the meanders of the trail you follow in, for no signs will be there to point your way out.

Should you choose to make the Nordhouse Dunes an overnight destination, camping is permitted with some restrictions. All water must be carried in and all garbage carried out. You'll find less rustic camping at the Lake Michigan Recreation Area, generally from May 15 to September 15.

How to get there: In Mason County, from US 31, about twelve miles south of Manistee, turn west on Town Line Road. Follow Town Line for 2.5 miles to Quarterline Road. Head north on Quarterline for two miles to Nurnberg Road. Take Nurnberg west for a little more than six miles to the parking lot at the trailheads. You can also gain access to the northern edge of the wilderness area from the Lake Michigan Recreation Area. To get to the recreation area, continue on Quarterline for 1.4 miles past Nurnberg. Then turn west on Forest Trail #5629, which leads to the parking area.

General information: Nordhouse Dunes Wilderness Area is open year-round. The Lake Michigan Recreation Area is open unless snowfall forces closure. For maps and other information, contact the Huron-Manistee National Forest, Manistee Ranger District, Manistee, MI 49660; 616-723-2211.

SAND LAKES QUIET AREA

Bikers, hikers, campers, and skiers who need to escape the crowds of Traverse City will appreciate the proximity of this attraction. Several small bodies of water are found here, but the five in the center are collectively called the "Sand Lakes." Lake #2 is a designated trout lake and attracts fishermen. Motorized vehicles are prohibited from the area, which includes several miles of trails, the longest loop being fifteen miles. Part of Michigan's Shore to Shore Riding/Hiking trail also passes through the southern edge.

You may see deer, wild turkeys, even a mama raccoon and her youngsters.

The biggest attraction of the Sand Lakes Quiet Area,

Young raccoons set off on thir own to explore the summer they're born

however, is the opportunity for primitive camping and semi-wilderness hiking and cross-country skiing with mostly nature's sounds to accompany you. While it's impossible to escape the drone of trucks and traffic even in some true wilderness areas, Sand Lakes grants about as much escape as you can hope for.

How to get there: In Grand Traverse/Kalkaska Counties, head east for 5.8 miles on M-72 from its junction with US 31 in Acme, east of Traverse City. Head south onto Broomhead Road for about one and a quarter miles to a crossroads. Turn east (left) and stay on the main dirt road until you reach the first parking area, about two and a half miles down the road. You can also continue past that parking area about an eighth of a mile to Island Lake

Road and turn left. Another parking area is seven-tenths of a mile down, on your right.

General information: The second parking area puts you closer to the trail leading to Lake #4, which has wells and pit toilets. Other than that, and the rustic camping facilities at Guernsey Lake in the area's extreme southeast corner, no other conveniences are provided. You must be self-reliant.

Island Lake Road is not plowed during winter.

For maps and other information, contact the DNR, Forest Management Division, Recreation and Trails Section, P.O. Box 30028, Lansing, MI 48909; 616-775-9727.

5

Upper Peninsula

INTRODUCTION

The fact that the Upper Peninsula is the only division in this book to get a separate introduction drops a big hint about the area's unique personality. This peninsula is so vast, so variable, so very special that it deserves special treatment. In fact, the case can be made that the whole Upper Peninsula itself is a "natural wonder." Needless to say, it must be considered an overnight destination. Take I-75 into Mackinaw City and take the Mackinac Bridge across the Straits of Mackinac. You're now in the Upper Peninsula.

To begin with, let's get our terms straight. "Northern Michigan" does not denote the Upper Peninsula. No, that term is used to indicate those areas that lie above the middle knuckles of the fingers in the mitten that is the Lower Peninsula. The glorious Upper Peninsula is the "U.P." (pronounced "yoo pee"). That must be why the natives up there are called "Yoopers." (Just in case you wonder, people from "down below" are sometimes called "flatlanders" or, because we live below the bridge, "trolls.")

You do the U.P. an injustice if you refer to it merely as "God's Country," the presence of a town called Paradise notwithstanding. It's more of "God's Cookie Jar" filled to the brim with a myriad of wondrous goodies to which you can treat yourself until you're ready to burst—then jam your hand back in and snatch some more.

Several features of the U.P., including two that have their own entries in this book, are so grand they have inspired entire books. More demure pleasures will come only through your own familiarity with and exploration of the U.P. The entries I have chosen for this section should give you a good idea of the endless diversion, activity, and serendipity that await you in to the U.P.

Actually, Mackinac (MACK-in-aw) Island does deserve an entry, but it is so overrun with tourists that I decided to skip it. If you can wait until after Labor Day, you will find the island less congested. Then too, you might feel more like renting a bicycle and exploring some of the natural features that became part of Native American legends, like Skull Cave and Arch Rock.

On your drives around Northern Michigan, you'll see tons of information inviting you to get to the island from Mackinaw City. If you are heading to the U.P. however, you should know that you can also reach the island via ferry service from St. Ignace. And as you take the sweeping curve at the top of the hill while heading toward downtown St. Ignace, pay attention to the park on your right and the gigantic rock that's been set there.

This is the American Legion Park, adjacent to the St. Ignace Chamber of Commerce and located on Moran Bay, which is part of the Straits Underwater Preserve. The rock is a nineteen-ton chunk of granite that displays a Michigan Heritage Memorial plaque. The plaque, placed by the Michigan Outdoor Writers Association, commemorates Great Lakes shipwrecks and Michigan's Underwater Preserves. Currently, the state has designated nearly 1,900 square miles as preserves in ten units, six of which are in the U.P. Another, a National Park Preserve, has been hed as a ring extending 4.5 miles from the shore of federally administered Isle Royale in the U.P. These preserves were established to protect popular diving sites from further salvaging, looting, or any type of artifact gathering or disturbance. This way, the wrecks will maintain their appeal for divers who come in from all around the United States.

Heading in the opposite direction from St. Ignace, about fifteen miles west of the bridge along US 2, which follows the Lake Michigan shoreline here, you'll find nearly five miles of splendid, accessible beaches. The road shoulders are extra wide, so you should have no trouble finding a spot when you're ready to pull over and enjoy the beach and dunes.

A little ways farther, 4.5 miles west of Brevort, you'll see turnoffs for the breathtaking view from the Cut River Bridge. You can enjoy things while picnicking up top or, if you feel up to the challenge, by taking the foot trail and descending nearly 200 feet to the river itself. And about seven miles west of the Cut River, you'll find another, though less magnificent, stretch of beaches.

Shifting attention to the northern coast of the U.P., if you like to camp under rustic conditions—pit toilets, water from pumps, no showers—be sure to explore the Lake Superior shoreline. Take a look at a county map book and you'll see several state and national forest rustic campgrounds dotting the shore route from just west of Sault Ste. Marie to Grand Marais.

You can set up your tent mere steps from the beach or you can pull in on a slab with your camper, *sans* electric hookups. The breeze will disperse the bugs. And the waves will lull you to sleep.

Another spot where you'll find several miles of roadside parks, picnic areas, and scenic turnouts (but no campsites) begins nine miles west of Munising, along M-28 at Lake Superior's Au Train Bay. From the opposite direction, the Marquette area, the stretch begins six miles east of the M-28/US 41 split.

In the upper tip of the ear of the running dog that is the U.P., Copper Harbor offers many diversions. For example, you can tour the Brockway Mountain Drive, once voted the most scenic in Michigan. In fact, the Keweenaw Peninsula has been rated as a top spot for observing raptor migrations in spring. Brockway Mountain Drive rises high enough and offers enough lookouts that you stand a good chance of watching bald eagles fly by at eye level. The migrations begin in March and dwindle after the first of May. Sometimes snow prevents access to the road until late April. Visitors interested in looking down instead of looking up can also search for their favorite stones along the beaches and pathways of the Keweenaw Peninsula. Rockhounds search for agates, Mohawkite, greenstone, even some copper remnants.

Throughout the U.P., hundreds of inland lakes and rivers beckon boaters and canoeists of all skill levels. Over 150 waterfalls await, some as obvious as Alger Falls, which almost tumbles into your lap as you enter Munising from the south on M-28. Others require various degrees of effort before rewarding you with a view. But there should be more than enough falls throughout the U.P. to sate even the most impassioned waterfall seekers.

If my name were "Whitman," I'd call this introduction my U.P. "Sampler." Even so, it doesn't even begin to scratch the surface of what awaits you, what invites you, what is sure to intrigue you if you have the time to get to know the place that's best described by the name chosen by Yoopers who would create the fifty-first state: "Superiorland."

For More Information

To get started on figuring an itinerary for a visit to the U.P., request a Travel Planner from the Upper Peninsula Travel and Recreation Association. Traditionally, one feature of the planner is a list of waterfalls by county, which should help you to plot side trips. Contact UPTRA, P.O. Box 400, Iron Mountain, MI 49801; 800-562-7134 or 906-774-5480.

Request Mackinac Island and Bottomland Preserve information from the St. Ignace Chamber of Commerce, 11 South State Street, St. Ignace, MI 49781; 800-338-6660 or 906-643-8717.

TAHQUAMENON FALLS STATE PARK

The second largest state park in Michigan, Tahquamenon extends over thirteen miles along the Taquamenon River and encompasses more than 35,000 acres. There's a simple reason you were routed to this spot, however. If you stop at no other area of the park, be sure to visit the upper falls.

If it weren't for Niagara's, these upper falls at Tahquamenon would be the largest east of the Mississippi, with a 200-foot-wide escarpment and a nearly 50-foot drop. The water flowing from the lowlands is rich in tannic acid from cedar and tamarack trees, so the river flows by in a deep, golden brown. At the brink of the falls where the foam begins, the river looks like root beer.

As you might expect, such a grandiose display by Mother Nature attracts a lot of attention from tourists. So if you don't like to be around a lot of people, plan to arrive early in the day, before the family groups can shake away the sleep, get organized, and hit the campground. On the other hand, the popularity of the upper falls led the state to install a pleasant boardwalk that runs from a stairway to the gorge, along the high banks, to a stairway to the brink of the falls.

At the lower falls, about four miles downstream, you can rent a boat to row to an island from where you can get a closer view. Or you can look from the riverbank. Two modern campsites are located at the lower falls.

The actual park continues even farther, to the mouth of the Tahquamenon River, nineteen miles from the upper falls by car. Here, you'll find both a modern and a rustic campground.

No camping is allowed at the upper falls.

You can actually hike from the upper falls all the way to the river mouth, taking a trail from the upper to the lower falls. From there to the river mouth, you'll pick up a portion of the North Country National Scenic Trail, which also passes through the park on the north side of M-123. You can make arrangements for backpack camping within the park.

And don't overlook the park in winter, when you'll find trails marked for snowmobiling and cross-country skiing. The falls often freeze over.

How to get there: In Luce/Chippewa Counties, a cockeyed triangle of highways is formed with east-west–running M-28 as its base and M-123 forming both sides as it loops north and creates an apex in Paradise. Take the west leg of M-123 north through the town of Newberry. Continue for another twenty-three miles to the entrance to the Upper Falls portion of the park.

General information: A motor vehicle permit is required for entry into the park. For information, contact the Manager, Tahquamenon Falls State Park, Star Route 48, P.O. Box 225, Paradise, MI 49768; 906-492-3415.

You can also try the Newberry Area Tourism Association, P.O. Box 308, Newberry, MI 49868; 800-831-7292. Or call the Newberry Area Chamber of Commerce, 906-293-5562.

WHITEFISH POINT BIRD OBSERVATORY (WPBO)

This is a wonderful place for viewing massive bird migrations in early spring and fall. During the remainder of warm weather, it's a great place to visit in order to find out what you missed.

Whitefish Point is an important enough bird-counting location to warrant a year-round staff. The most spectacular time for viewing birds, however, is the last week of April and the first two weeks of May. This is the usual time for the hawks and other raptors to appear. Observatory workers can usually figure on counting 15,000 to 23,000 raptors each spring.

And we're not just talking about singletons or a few pairs at a time. Flocks. Dozens of birds. Enough to cause the counter on the observation deck to radio the office attendant and tell her to "look at those giant mosquitoes!" swarming past the office window.

Depending on the luck of the draw, you may see high numbers of any of several types of raptors: northern harriers, red-tailed hawks, American kestrels, sharp-shinned hawks, even ospreys or bald eagles. This glorious display of migrating birds of prey is in addition to the dozens of species of songbirds and nine owl species that pass by. Curiously enough, these land birds are not the only types to be seen at the WPBO. Over 300 species have been identified at one time or another, and that also includes waterfowl and shorebirds such as common loons, grebes, cormorants, and sandhill cranes. In fact, Whitefish Point itself is a nesting area for the endangered piping plover as well as other shorebirds, and the Coast Guard has restricted entry and activities in the area.

If the Lower Peninsula can be described as a mitten, then the Upper is a dog running westward. With that in mind, consider Whitefish Point as the short tail of the dog. And except for the extended rear legs, this tail is the closest point between Michigan's U.P. and Canada. This is an important factor that explains the attraction of Whitefish Point for migrating birds, both those that are basically landlubbers and birds of the water.

Land birds don't like to cross wide expanses of water. As a result, through time, the birds have learned that if they fly up through the Lower Peninsula and Wisconsin and then follow the

U.P. to Whitefish Point, they will have the narrowest crossing to their nesting grounds in Canada. On the other hand, waterfowl and shorebirds prefer the open water. They fly up Lake Huron and the straits between Huron and Superior and continue to head to the open water of Lake Superior. Whitefish Point is a natural spot for them to congregate.

Even though the beach area is part of the Coast Guard's regulated piping plover nesting habitat, you are still free to roam the sandy expanse that awaits you. Also, as part of a restoration project, a short boardwalk passes over some of the sensitive dune area. The boardwalk leads to an observation deck and the enclosed station where the bird counter sits during migrations. From there you can marvel at your view of the dunes and grasses, Whitefish Bay, and Lake Superior. But you better not bother the bird counter!

The northern migrations last from late March to mid-June. The southern migrations begin in August and last until mid-November.

In addition to the charts listing species and numbers of bird sighted, the observatory station also maintains a small interpretive center. While there, be sure to note the display of the various sizes of leg bands used on the various sizes of birds. At the WPBO, the primary focus is on the banding of the hawks, falcons, and owls.

Don't be surprised when you arrive at Whitefish Point to find several other buildings and even a gift shop other than the one in the bird observatory. The point is also remembered as the location of Lake Superior's first lighthouse, built in 1849.

Great Lakes Shipwreck Historical Museum

I know I said this book would emphasize nature and not human history, but every now and again I have to make an exception.

Nowhere is an exception more appropriate than with this museum, which is located at Whitefish Point. For in no other way in Michigan is human history more a pawn in nature's hand than when we take to the inland seas. And nowhere in Michigan do the inland seas exact more tribute from their subjects than in the Whitefish Point area, also called the "Graveyard of the Great Lakes."

This is the graveyard because of all the shipwrecks in the area. One exhibit at the museum says that shipwrecks combine the romance of the lakes with the violence of nature in ways people simply find fascinating. This small museum, erected in 1987, gives just enough information, through text, artifacts, and a wonderfully effective full-size diorama of divers on the hull of the *Independence*, either to tease such fascination or to subdue it.

The history of wrecks in the area is covered through representative displays, from the first wreck, the *Invincible*, in 1816; to Amos Stiles, "the man who never smiled again," after his experience on the *Independence* in 1853; to the *Edmund Fitzgerald*, which went down in November 1975.

Make no mistake: the *Edmund Fitzgerald* is the focal point of the museum. The suggested route through its one room leads to the *Fitzgerald* display, which includes some flotsam, among which, eerily enough, is a life ring. It also includes transcripts from some of the final radio transmissions between the *Fitzgerald* and the *Anderson*, the ship closest to it when it went down. Before you head over to the Shipwreck Theatre to see the *Fitzgerald* video, stop to consider the list of names of the ill-fated the crew while, in the background, Gordon Lightfoot sings, "the church bell chimed till it rang twenty-nine times for each man on the *Edmund Fitzgerald*."

How to get there: In Chippewa County, from M-28 take the east leg of M-123 north for twenty-two miles to the town of Paradise. Instead of turning west and staying on M-123 at the blinking light in town, remain northbound on the road, which becomes White-fish Point Road. Follow it until it dead-ends eleven miles later at the U.S. Coast Guard property where the observatory sits on the shores of Lake Superior.

General information: The observatory station is open to the public from mid-April to the end of October. The museum is open seven days a week from Memorial Day to mid-October. Your paid admission to the museum also gets you into the theater.

For an idea of all the species of birds you might see, get a copy of a "Checklist to the Birds of Whitefish Point Bird Observatory." Contact the observatory for the current cost: WPBO, HC 48, Box 115, Paradise, MI 49768; 906-492-3596.

SENEY NATIONAL WILDLIFE REFUGE

I like the agreeable crunch of the gravel on a graded road when I'm driving slowly with no particular ends in mind. Apparently, the hawk didn't find the massive gray steel intruder that is our Suburban to be as agreeable. As I drove further into the woods, it sneaked up, swooping low from behind us to almost eye level in the windshield, then veered into the woods before I could note any field marks. No way to tell if it were nearsighted and figured we were a mouse sneaking down the road, if it saw something more delectable beyond the road, or if it felt it had given us a good, stiff warning. No matter. That counts as a wildlife encounter.

You can just about predict some kind of a wildlife encounter when you visit the Seney National Wildlife Refuge, one of only two such refuges in the state that have headquarters and staffs who can answer your questions. If nothing else, you'll have to step carefully from the parking lot to the visitors center so you can avoid the Canada geese—and their mementos.

In fact, before you set out on your own to explore the 95,000-plus acres that comprise the refuge, you probably should pay a visit to the visitors center. There, you'll find a number of exhibits and displays, all meant to acquaint you with the animals of the area. These displays and the various workshops and programs given by the staff are geared especially to children.

The center houses mounted specimens and some skeletons of animals. Always a popular item, the "touch table" is set up at kid level. You can also check out the sounds of birds and study the wetlands display.

The visitors center overlooks one of the ponds in the refuge, a sight that urges you outside to try to see what you've learned about inside.

What's special about the Seney refuge is that you have a choice of modes of transportation.

Hikers will find the 1.4-mile looped Pine Ridge Nature Trail starting just outside the visitors center. That trail gives you a quick introduction to the habitat, plants, and wildlife of the refuge, which is located in the Great Manistique Swamp.

Those who prefer to get a feel for the land from the comfort of their automobile will want to drive the seven-mile, self-guided Marshland Wildlife Drive. At several spots along the trail, you can pull off to better observe the birds you see in the ponds. And be careful to watch for smaller species, like the eastern kingbird, which may be nesting in the tall weeds of the marshes. You'll also find three observation decks, from which you may spot the trumpeter swans, loons, ospreys, sandhill cranes, or bald eagles, among the 200 species of birds that have been seen in the park. Nearly fifty species of mammals have also been listed, among which are the occasional timber wolf or moose. The Marshland Drive is open from May through October.

The refuge is also open for cross-country skiing and snowshoeing. Trails are groomed from mid-December to mid-March.

Perhaps of all the spots mentioned in this book, this is the best place for pure, unadulterated, "no one's gonna' yell at you or run you off the road with something bigger" mountain biking. Throughout the refuge, bikers will find nearly seventy miles of roads available to them that are otherwise closed to motor vehicles. As one staff member told me, "If you are on the refuge and you come to a locked gate over a road, just lift your bike over the gate." You may even find yourself on a gravel road with a hawk as your copilot.

How to get there: In Schoolcraft County, from US 2, take M-77 north about twelve miles to the entrance of the refuge. From the town of Seney, take M-77 south about five miles.

General information: While the refuge is open year-round, the visitors center is open only from May 15 to September 30, seven days a week, from 9:00 A.M. to 5:00 P.M. There is no admission charge.

For more information, bicycle trail maps, and schedules of interpretive programs, contact Seney National Wildlife Refuge, HCR2, Box 1, Seney, MI 49883; 906-586-9851.

GRAND ISLAND NATIONAL RECREATION AREA

That the roadside parks along Lake Superior end at Grand Marais and begin again just west of Munising did not happen by coincidence. Extending east to west for about forty miles between Grand Marais and Munising is Pictured Rocks, America's first National Lakeshore, a place of rugged terrain and unparalleled beauty. No shoreline highways here, for they would destroy what makes this area beautiful.

You can't consult any U.P. vacation magazines or pamphlets without being directed toward Pictured Rocks. Small wonder. There is so much to do here that a simple listing should whet your appetite enough that you'll want to find out more on your own. Hiking, backcountry camping, sea kayaking, car touring, and cross-country skiing are a few of the activities you can enjoy. To get a taste of the spot, you must make it an overnight destination.

You'll see beautiful stands of white birch trees, four miles of sand dunes, and at least nine waterfalls within a half hour's drive of Munising. A short walk from one parking lot brings you to an overlook of the rock formation known as "Miners Castle." The main feature of the National Lakeshore, the view of the Pictured Rocks, can really be enjoyed only from the water, and most tourists won't be towing their own boats with them. A concession offering viewing cruises of the rocks operates out of Munising.

So I can trust the travel brochures to sell you on the idea of a visit to the Pictured Rocks.

That frees me to talk about Grand Island, a diamond in the rough perched dazzlingly close to the Pictured Rocks and Munising, so close as to entice you for a visit.

The Grand Island National Recreation Area has been so recently established that the management plan for its development has yet to be finalized and implemented. Even so, this many-faceted gem is currently available for the pleasure of Upper Peninsula visitors.

The 13,558-acre island is about eight miles long and three miles across at its widest point. With a shoreline of twenty-six miles, it can be a real treat for semi-serious backpackers who want to follow a circular route. Hiking is just one of the activities for visitors to Grand Island.

A 1990 law created the National Recreation Area "to preserve and protect for present and future generations the outstanding resources and values" and "for conservation protection and enhancement of its scenery, recreation, fish and wildlife, vegetation, and historical and cultural resources."

Make no mistake, Grand Island is a "special land." From

**Peregrine falcons are spectacular flyers, plummeting
at 180 miles an hour to catch flying birds**

the enigma it presents to geologists trying to determine its formation, to the regenerating hardwoods replacing what the lumbermen took, to the bays and beaches, the island sings a siren song to the pilgrim. It's a sandstone outcrop with cliffs as high as 300 feet at its northern end. It contains six ecosystem types: poor and rich conifer swamps, mixed pine forests, pine-hardwood forests, hemlock-hardwood forests, and rich northern hardwoods.

While no endangered plant species have been identified, several threatened and "special concern" plants have been found. A bald eagle nests on the island. Loons can sometimes be seen on Echo Lake at the heart of the island. And peregrine falcons have been identified on and around the island. That is to be expected, for as part of a reintroduction program, the Pictured Rocks area was the scene of peregrine falcon releases from 1989 to 1991. Ruffed grouse, white-tailed deer, and black bear are the most prominent wildlife species on the island.

As of this writing, there is little restriction on use of the island. ATVs are allowed on maintained and unmaintained dirt roads. The trails are set aside for hikers and mountain bikers alone. No wheeled vehicles are allowed on the beaches—foot traffic only. While bikes are allowed on the commercial passenger ferry from Munising, getting ATVs to the island may be a problem, for no public docking exists. Private boaters must anchor or moor in Murray Bay.

Currently, campers are restricted in only a few ways: to camp near the beaches on Murray Bay or Trout Bay, they must use designated campsites; also, no camping is allowed at North Beach or near buildings. Otherwise, campers are welcome to set up anyplace on the island. And they are well advised to take precautions against bears by hanging their food caches from trees and keeping food out of tents.

For four years an advisory commission considered eight different development plans for Grand Island. In July 1994, the supervisor of Hiawatha National Forest proposed a "Selected Alternative" for Grand Island. Under this plan, ATVs will be banned from the northeast portion of the island and its "thumb." These areas will be set aside for backpackers, bikers, and hunters. No more than eighteen miles of "hiking only" trails will be complemented by up to thirty miles of "bike/hike" trails. The thumb will be an area for hiking only. Permits will be required for all camping.

A natural area of nearly sixty acres already exists in the northwest portion of the island. Under the proposed plan, this area will remain pretty much a natural setting similar to the northeast and the thumb, except less adventurous travelers will be able to visit by taking the public transportation from the south.

During winter use, fifty miles of designated snowmobile trails are planned for parts of the main island and the "tombolo," or stretch of land connecting the thumb to the island. The entire island will be available to cross-country skiers and snowshoers.

No matter how much this gem becomes cut and fitted to man's designs, it is still set in Lake Superior and must be regarded with caution. "The use period of Grand Island," says U.S. Park Service representative Julie Fosbender, "ranges from late April to early November. During spring ice breakup and winter freeze-up the island is inaccessible." National Forest pamphlets advise visitors of the unpredictable nature of Lake Superior and that they should be prepared to spend at least one extra night on the island "if foul weather erupts."

Also, winter recreationists are warned that while snow-mobiling, cross-country skiing, and snowshoeing are permitted on the island, changing ice conditions and underwater currents sometimes make crossing the strait treacherous. As with using many of the trails on the island and beaches along the Pictured Rocks National Lakeshore, crossing on the ice is a "travel at your own risk" proposition.

Finally, you should know that you must be entirely self-sufficient when you visit the island. No drinking water is available; you must bring your own or filter surface water. Bugs are bad from mid-May through mid-July. And during summer, the ferry makes only two trips a day, morning and early evening. So you must be able to entertain yourself all day long.

A trip to Grand Island will show you one gem that sparkles on its own, with no need of a man-made setting.

How to get there: In Alger County, Grand Island is located in Lake Superior, about half a mile out from the city of Munising.
General information: Request Grand Island information and exhaustive Pictured Rocks info from the Hiawatha National Forest, Munising District Office, 400 East Munising, Munising, MI 49862; 906-387-3700.

You can also contact the National Park Headquarters at P.O. Box 40, Munising, MI 49862; 906-387-2607.

You should be able to request diverse literature, from an official map and guide to the National Lakeshore, to pamphlets on activities and features like back-country camping, cross-country ski trails, waterfalls, day hikes, peregrine falcons, and sea kayaking, for example. Be sure to request a current copy of the park's tabloid, *Lakeshore Observer,* which, in addition to little news stories about park features, lists the season's interpretive programs.

Pictured Rocks Cruises Inc. offers the viewing trips of the Pictured Rocks and operates the passenger ferry to Grand Island. For fares and schedules, call 906-387-2379. Expect to pay extra for any bicycles you take along.

For even more information on the area in general, try contacting the Chamber of Commerce, P.O. Box 139, Grand Marais, MI 49839; 906-494-2612. Also the Alger Chamber of Commerce, P.O. Box 405, Munising, MI 49862; 906-387-2138.

MARQUETTE COUNTRY

If Marquette, the largest city in the U.P., is your base, the main highway is a junction of US 41/M-28. For ease, in this section, I'll just refer to it as "41."

Rest assured, an entire book could be written about the Marquette area of the U.P. itself. Indeed, it has, and it is two volumes and over a thousand pages long. So you can rest doubly assured that the few attractions I'll mention merely serve as an enticement. Certainly, you'll want to mine the depths of possibilities yourself.

It's appropriate to consider your explorations of the area as "mining," for Marquette is the gateway to "Iron Country" in the U.P. If you approach from Munising, the view of Marquette gets bumpier and bumpier as the hills of the iron mines rise from the plains you've just crossed. The terrain gets even more hilly as the nearby Huron Mountains and eventually the hills of Copper Country on the Keweenaw Peninsula rise northwest of Marquette, and the Porcupine Mountains rise to the southwest. Another sign that you've entered another world: at this stage, you are so far from the population bulges of southeastern Michigan that the Green Bay Packers and Milwaukee Brewers are considered the home teams.

As far as cultural history goes, therefore, the mines have played an integral part in the development of the area. History says that 40 percent of the iron ore for the Industrial Revolution came from Marquette County and that nearby Negaunee was once the richest city in the world.

Of course, where you find hills you will also find valleys, streams, and waterfalls. Inland lakes and reservoirs also complement the miles of Lake Superior shoreline awaiting you in the Marquette area. In short, if you love the outdoors, Marquette offers year-round recreational opportunities. With spring comes the emergence of wildflowers and morels, plus the return of migrating birds and renewed activity of larger mammals. Summer brings berries, lush vegetation and water sports. The fall color of the area is legendary. And even though the northern route into Marquette—M-28 from Munising—can sometimes be closed by blizzards, recreation does not stop during the long U.P. winters. Cross-country ski trails abound. You'll also find alpine skiing plus both a luge and a toboggan hill near to town.

It would be tough to convince first-time visitors that Marquette is an outdoors lover's idea of Nirvana based on what they'd see along 41. As the commercial center of the U.P., home to a major university, and the capital for the semi-seriously proposed fifty-first state of "Superiorland," Marquette—at least on the edges—has that "medium-big city" look about it. But you don't have to meander too far from 41 to find something else.

Presque Isle Park

From downtown Marquette, take Fourth Street north. Its name will change to Presque Isle. Drive past Northern Michigan University's indoor sports arena, affectionately known as the "Yooperdome." Turn right onto Hawley, then left onto Lakeshore Boulevard. This road will take you into the park.

In French, *Presque Isle* means "nearly an island," and a glance at a map will show you why. If Italy looks like a foot preparing to kick the soccer ball that is Sicily, then Presque Isle Park resembles an upright foot following through on such a kick.

This 328-acre city park is a microcosm of all that the Marquette area has to offer. It's close to town yet has magnificent natural features.

You can drive the two-mile loop for a quick view. Three other hike/ski trails embrace a total of about three miles covering flat to slightly hilly terrain, rated as "moderate." Just outside the entrance to the park, you'll also find the Bog Walk, an easy, quarter-mile trail that is wheelchair accessible.

There's a simple, obvious reason why the northern tip of the park—the "big toe" of this foot-is called Sunset Point. As at Mallory Square in Key West, Florida, nature's biggest draw on humans here is the spectacle each evening when the sun bids a glorious farewell.

To the west, Sugarloaf Mountain is closest to the shoreline. Hogsback Mountain sports the two tips.

Sugarloaf Mountain

Wright Street runs west from Presque Isle then south to 41. County 550 begins at Wright about half a mile west of Presque Isle, or 3.2 miles from 41. You want to take County Road 550 north for about five miles to get to Sugarloaf Mountain's parking area.

Some Easter Sunday, I'm going to set out for Sugarloaf's peak about twenty-five minutes before sunrise. Just to get into the spirit of things.

You've got about a half-mile climb, mostly stairway, to get to the peak, 315 feet above the surrounding landscape. If you aren't used to physical exertion, take your time. You'll be glad you did when you view the panorama including Lake Superior, the town of Marquette, and to the south a seemingly endless expanse of forests and other hills.

You can actually hike to and from the peak along trails that are part of the Little Presque Isle Tract. This area of over 3,000 acres takes you along Lake Superior's shore, through the woods, back to Harlow Lake, and up Hogsback Mountain. Except for the climb to Hogsback, which is rated as "moderately difficult to steep," the rest of the trail is rated as "moderate."

This attraction typifies best the wonderful dichotomy that

is Marquette: on these trails you must consider yourself in an actual survival situation while at the same time you remain within about five miles of a major city.

On the south side of County 550, about half a mile past the parking area for Sugarloaf, you'll find the entrance to the Wetmore Landing parking area, from which you can take your choice of trails that lead into the woods. One heads up Hogsback, another to the lakeshore.

Moose Viewing

Until 1985, the only moose remaining in Michigan were those that were holed up on Isle Royale, fifty miles from the mainland U.P. Then, through an extraordinary effort known as Operation Moose Lift, adult moose were captured in Ontario, blindfolded, hoisted in slings hanging from helicopters, crated at awaiting trucks, transported to Marquette County, and released. A second moose lift took place in 1987.

A total of fifty-nine moose were released. The 1994 summer estimate placed the herd size at 304. Needless to say, the moose are a big attraction here, so you need to be prepared to view them.

Step one includes a trip to Lindquist's Outdoor Sports on Washington Street in downtown Marquette. There, you'll see two mounted moose heads on the wall. Mosey on up to the bigger of the two, nod in its direction, and ask with familiarity if not authority, "That one John Weber's?" The clerk will think you know my buddy Web.

Step two is a stop at Jilbert's Dairy. As you head west on 41 out of town, you'll see the big red barn on your right. The store there is like the local dairy's version of a factory outlet. Get a nice big helping of Jilbert's "Moose Tracks" ice cream. Just to

**Two out of three moose mothers give birth to twins,
sometimes even to triplets**

keep the mood going as you head out on a longer leg of your journey.

Step three is a drive to Van Riper State Park.

The park is located about thirty miles west of Marquette with its entrance off 41.

Your focal point here is the moose information kiosk, which carries updated moose information/statistics boards. It also contains a map on which magnets are moved to show most recent locations of moose. Schedule enough time there to watch the fourteen-minute video of the saga of Operation Moose Lift and read the commemorative Michigan Heritage Memorial Plaque placed by the Michigan Outdoor Writers Association.

The reason I instructed you to begin this tour by looking at mounted moose is simple. No one can predict exactly where you'll need to travel and when in order to see one on your tour. You can request a pamphlet of suggested routes to follow where animals are often seen, but even it carries a reminder that there are no guarantees. You're just as apt to see a moose crossing the highway in the middle of the day as you are to view one while searching for them.

As with most animals, the best time to see moose is in the early morning or evening. Look for them to be feeding on aquatic plants along the edges of bogs, ponds, lakes, or streams. They may also be seen in stands of young aspen.

Hills Falls

I decided not to "waterfalls" you to boredom in the U.P. section of the book. I do, however, want to include one of the nineteen in the Marquette area, and my selection was determined by the fact that the route you take to get here is also one Greg Hokans told me he'd take if he wanted to increase his chances of seeing moose. It's route number 6 in the "Moose Locator Guide" published by the Marquette Country Convention and Visitors Bureau, where Greg is executive director.

About five miles west of Marquette, just past the sign for the "Midway Industrial Park," from 41 turn north (right) onto Midway Drive (County 502). At the sign that says "McLure Dam/ Hoist Dam," bear to the right. (Midway will curve to the left, forming a crescent and eventually returning to 41. So if you end up back on the highway, you missed the second turn.) You now should be on County 510. Take 510 about twenty miles to the steel bridge that crosses the Yellow Dog River.

And watch out for moose on your drive!

Once you park near the bridge, you'll see the trail to the falls on the north side of the road. At a brisk pace, it's about a ten-minute walk back to Hills Falls. On the way in, stick to the right when the trail branches. (On the way out, stick to the left.)

Along the trail, I saw a forty-foot-tall aspen that a beaver, apparently, had given up working on. If it's still there for your walk, you will be about two minutes from the falls.

There are a couple of simple reasons I included these falls. First, you have to make an effort to get to them. That means you stand a better chance for solitude than you would at a falls people can drive right up to. Also, they're kind of neat, almost look manageable compared to Tahquamenon or some of the other big falls you can visit. Although the Hills Falls look tame, manageable, and inviting, however, the rocks beneath the water are treacherously slick.

The above ideas barely scratch the surface of the treasures that await you in the Marquette area. Remember, the mining is up to you.

General information: For maps of area hiking trails, including the Little Presque Isle Tract, contact the DNR's Ishpeming Field Office, 1985 US 41 West, Ishpeming, MI 49849; 906-485-1031. Ask for maps of the Presque Isle Forest Recreation Area. Also, if you favor canoes or boats, ask for a map of nearby Greenwood Reservoir, a wilderness lake with over thirty miles of shoreline but only one boat launch about five miles down County 478 off US 41.

If you have any inkling at all that you might like to visit, by all means contact the Marquette Country Convention and Visitors Bureau. The people there are the most helpful I've ever encountered—whether planning trips myself or in helping me gather information for this book. Give them your address plus an idea of what activities or features you are interested in and what time of year you'll visit, and sit back and wait for the mail. And don't forget to ask for your "Moose Locator Guide."

Contact the Marquette Country Convention and Visitors Bureau, 2552 US 41 West, Suite 300, Marquette, MI 49855; 800-544-4321 or 906-228-7749.

McCORMICK WILDERNESS

For the first half of the twentieth century, McCormick Wilderness was the private holding of the family of Cyrus McCormick, son of the inventor of the reaper. They used the camp as a retreat for themselves and for their employees at the International Harvester Company. In 1967, the property was willed to the U.S. Government by Gordon McCormick, grandson of the reaper's inventor. In 1987, it became part of the National Wilderness Preservation System.

Freed from the lumberman's saw since the early 1900s, the McCormick Tract (16,850 acres – about twenty-seven square miles) has had a chance to reestablish itself as a wilderness with a variety of forest types. The U.S. Forest Service reports that northern hardwoods cover about 47 percent of the area, with a heavy mixture of hardwoods and conifers, including pine. The report also estimates that 86 percent of the area contains trees that are 120 years old or older. Virgin pine still exists in a few small stands.

The topography varies from flat lands to rocky outcrops, from uplands to swamps and muskegs. Except for the trail leading from the entrance off County 607 to White Deer Lake, most other trails have become overgrown. The trail to White Deer Lake actually had been a road, used by the McCormicks and their guests for driving back to the camps built on the mainland and a small island in the lake.

With most evidence of development removed by man or reclaimed by nature, the McCormick Tract remains a draw for serious connoisseurs of wilderness areas. The area is open to foot traffic only, and even Forest Service workers perform only "walk-in maintenance." More rugged and experienced explorers might think of making this a destination for a backcountry camping adventure.

In winter, "foot traffic" means snowshoes or cross-country skis. Sometimes, however, County 607 doesn't get plowed, and would-be sojourners into the wilderness can't make the 9.5-mile drive to the entrance trail. And if the trail is passable, chances are you'd be better off with your snowshoes than with skis. It is not groomed. In fact, except for the main trail, which is identified by a sign alongside the county road, other trails are user located and user maintained.

Both the sky and the roads are clear today, and with our trustworthy *negaunee* in charge, we'll need no signs to find our way through the McCormick Wilderness.

Negaunee is the Ojibwa word for "one who goes first," according to Fred Rydholm, Marquette area historian. Having guided in the general area for thirty years, he is certainly prepared to lead the way, both by giving directions and by recounting the history.

And so, we're off.

The wilderness seems so desolate you're tempted to think nothing lives here. But the myriad tracks that cross the main trail belie that outlook. An experienced woodsman can interpret the dramas that have been played out since the last snow. The wilderness plays host to white-tailed deer, black bears, otters, foxes, coyotes, mink, squirrels, and snowshoe hares. In spring, the muddy banks of White Deer and Bulldog Lakes are covered with coyote tracks.

This is also the area where thirty moose were released in 1987, the second release of moose that were airlifted from the

Canadian wilderness. Pine marten, too, have been reintroduced.

Most of the confirmed mountain lion sightings in the U.P. have taken place in the general vicinity of McCormick. Fishers have been seen in the area, and a lynx was shot nearby, not long ago.

For being so diversely populated, though, the area is remarkably quiet. We can't hear much but the rhythmic swishing of our snowshoes and Rydholm's voice as we penetrate deeper into the wilderness.

Ultimately, it's the kind of quiet that lets you know that, in no uncertain terms, nature is in charge here. You'd do well to avoid challenging her; the closest thing to victory that you could hope for is a spanking.

Forest Service documents spell things out in more specific terms: "The opportunity for solitude is excellent because the area is remote and its periphery has poor access. . . . The area offers some physical and mental challenge during the summer and winter months because of its rugged character and overall lack of development including trails. The weather in all seasons adds an extra dimension to this challenge, especially during the winter months."

On the right, the outcrops rise so steeply and with such dominance that you quickly dismiss the notion that you'd like to partake in an impromptu rock climbing session. Instead, you turn to the left from the trail, through the lowlands toward an opening.

No question now that you are in the Upper Peninsula in the middle of winter. The bright sun, a false friend that convinced you to leave your scarf in the van, sends its Judas wind down the chute at the spreads of Baraga Creek. It's now the wind's turn to cackle as it takes a few bites from where your scarf should be. You hasten to complete your side trip and hit the protected trail, heading back toward the car.

The trail is little more than three miles long, so the six-mile round-trip should prove to be an easy hike for a person in moderate shape. This is especially true if he allows for many rest stops either to take a drink or snack, or read animal tracks, contemplate plant life, or listen for an animal that might decide to crack the wilderness's code of silence.

On your way from the trail to the parking area, take another look at the sign that identifies the spot. It's hard to believe that such a common, seemingly insignificant Forest Service marker serves as the gateway to such a garden of backcountry delights.

How to get there: In Marquette County, from Marquette, take US 41/ M-28 west about fifty miles. About a mile west of Van Riper State Park, after crossing the Peshekee River Bridge, turn north (right) on County 607, also called "Peshekee Grade," then "Huron Bay Grade." Stay on 607 for about 9.5 miles. Watch on the right for the U.S. Forest Service sign reading "McCormick Wilderness." The parking lot is not plowed during winter.

General information: You can get a rudimentary map of the McCormick Tract as well as other trails in the Marquette Country from the DNR, Ishpeming Field Office, 1985 US 41 West, Ishpeming, MI 49849; 906-485-1031.

For more in-depth information, contact the Ottawa National Forest, East US 2, Ironwood, MI 49938; 800-562-1201 or 906-932-1330.

DeVRIENDT NATURE TRAIL

Visitors on their way to "Copper Country" might want to plan to stop at this easy-to-visit roadside attraction consisting of various wetland habitats and the wildlife they attract. The DeVriendt Nature Trail is located in the Sturgeon River Sloughs State Wildlife Refuge, the spot where the Sturgeon River spreads before emptying into Portage Lake.

This area attracts many diverse types of wildlife, including nesting waterfowl such as Canada geese, blue-winged teal, mallards, wood ducks, and black ducks. You may also see sandhill cranes, red-winged blackbirds, kestrels, great blue herons, rough-legged hawks, bald eagles, ospreys, and American bitterns. Mammals that have been spotted in this area include white-tailed deer, beavers, otters, black bears, coyotes, and red foxes.

A viewing platform beside the parking area offers a nice vantage for observing the different birds as they flutter around and drop into the ponds in the spring and fall. In summer, you might want to take a stroll along the self-guided interpretive trail. Although the trail is only about a mile long, allow at least forty-five minutes to work your way from signpost to signpost, understanding what is explained, observing what you can, and imagining what you can't, as the ponds give way to a swamp and the trail eventually leads back to the Sturgeon River just above its mouth. Before returning, you might want to take a breather at the rest bench and just watch the world, or at least the river, drift by.

An interesting man-made feature of the area is the "Donut Ponds," which were created to give waterfowl desirable nesting areas. The ponds were dug in the 1940s when it was realized that the natural banks were too steep to allow desirable vegetation to grow and also too restrictive in the visibility they offered the nesting birds. The hole of each donut is a little island mound; the donut itself is the water that encircles the mound, thus preventing land-based predators from sneaking up on the nesting female.

The flats upon which these ponds sit give way to a marshland that visitors cross via a boardwalk. The last leg of the trail traverses a section of secondary-growth timber such as white pine, white birch, northern red oak, and red maple. Knowledgeable hikers will also be able to identify several types of berries in the area and wildflowers, which line the sides of the paths.

Otters groom each other so their thick fur can keep them warm and dry

How to get there: On US 41 about two miles south of the town of Chassel (in Houghton County). You can't miss the sign for DeVriendt on the east side of the road.

ISLE ROYALE NATIONAL PARK

A feeling of awe overcame me when I placed my fist inside the track. The track was so large that my closed hand fit neatly inside with about an inch to spare all the way around. A feeling of concern overcame me when I realized that the game path I had meandered onto was just wide enough to accommodate one perturbed moose, not a moose and a hiker. A feeling of relief washed over me when I stepped back onto the main trail, having successfully avoided the feeling of stupidity that would have accompanied an encounter with whatever was grunting its way closer to me on the game trail. A feeling of envy arose when I returned to camp only to learn from my friend Danny that a red fox had moseyed through the campground during my absence.

Until the moose release near Marquette in 1985, Isle Royale was the only spot in Michigan where you could catch a glimpse of a moose. And until gray wolves reintroduced themselves to the mainland in the mid-1980s, Isle Royale was the only spot in Michigan where you could catch a glimpse of wolves. The isolated nature of the island made it a perfect laboratory for studying the predator-prey relationship between the two animals. In fact, so much of the island has been spared the touch of man that 99 percent of the park's land area is designated as wilderness, and Isle Royale has also been designated as an international biosphere reserve under the Man and the Biosphere (MAB) program.

Perched out there near the western shores of Lake Superior, Isle Royale rises as part of the Keweenaw series, the same billion-year-old Precambrian era volcanic rock that forms the base of the Porcupine Mountains on the mainland. Its many coves and inlets—Isle Royale has 600 miles of waterways—make it a dream destination for boaters. Lake Superior is so cold and the warmer, inland lakes so leech-infested that the National Park Service discourages swimming. The lake can summon enough bad weather to alter your day's plans drastically. In fact, if you plan to take with you a boat smaller than twenty feet long, the Park Service recommends you ferry it and yourself to the island via one of the commercial boats. There's also a chance that bad weather will prevent you from returning to the mainland on time—or at least not according to the schedule you have set; nature can do that, you know. Backpackers and hikers must be totally self-sufficient. Water from lakes and streams must be boiled for at least five minutes before you drink it; chemical purification will not kill the bacteria or the eggs of the hydatid tapeworm that are in the water. Hikers are advised not to roam cross-country or off-trail because of the many bogs and areas of thick vegetation. The closest thing to creature comforts campers will find are the eighty-six three-sided shelters that are located throughout the park. Blackflies and mosquitoes are guaranteed to time the peak of their visit with yours; be sure to bring along plenty of bug dope. There's no public phone service available on the island. Nor is there medical service. And you just might run into a moose that isn't very happy to see you.

So much for the wilderness and isolation.

Visitors desiring more accommodating accommodations, however, can reserve rooms or housekeeping cabins at the Rock Harbor Lodge, a concession run through the National Park system. Like the growing season in the U.P., the tourist season at Isle Royale is very short, running from early June to early September.

Several nature walks and evening slide programs are offered through the ranger station in Rock Harbor, as well as boat tours to different areas of the island. Also, for backpackers who want to see as much new territory as their time on Isle Royale will allow, there's a one-way boat taxi service that will drop you off at your choice of several points along the way so that your entire hike is a return to Rock Harbor instead of a loop from and toward it. The marina also rents small motorboats and canoes for those who want to poke around the shorelines on their own.

Over 166 miles of foot trails offer hikers and backpackers a myriad of choices during their visit. The Greenstone Ridge Trail runs the length of the island from Rock Harbor to Windigo Inn.

**Gray wolves have swum across from Isle Royale
and begun to repopulate the mainland**

While there's a store and boat rentals at Windigo, there is no lodge. Sprinkled along the island are thirty-one trailside and lakeside campgrounds.

Historically, Isle Royale has provided for mankind in several ways. The island's copper was mined by Native Americans and later the Europeans. The ruins of some mines are still visible along the trails. The French came there for furs. Europeans also logged the land for its fine lumber, then used it as a base for commercial fishing. And by the early 1900s, Isle Royale became a popular destination for summer vacationers.

You'll see a mixture of tree species on Isle Royale. While mixed evergreen species populate the moist shores and lake borders, hardwood stands have taken root in the interior and upland regions. And despite its short growing season, Isle Royale plays host to over 100 species of wildflowers.

While moose are often seen here, the same cannot be said for white-tailed deer. The only way for mammals to get to the island is to negotiate the stretch of water that is most narrow between Canada and the island. The moose probably swam from Canada while the timber wolves crossed on the ice bridge that was formed during the winter of 1948–49. Deer were introduced to the island but died out. More than 200 species of birds have been sighted from the island.

How to get there: In Keweenaw County, Isle Royale is seventy-three miles from Houghton, fifty-six from Copper Harbor. Commercial boat service from Houghton and Copper Harbor. Air taxi from Houghton. The marina at Rock Harbor can accommodate private boats up to sixty-five feet long.

General information: All campers must get a camping permit from the ranger station at Rock Harbor. The permit merely allows you to camp; it neither reserves nor guarantees a spot in a sleeping shelter or at a campsite. Campers need to know that outside of main campgrounds they may use only gas or alcohol stoves; no hard fuels or open wood fires. Bottles, cans, and other nonburnable disposables are prohibited from the backcountry.

The park is open from about mid-May to mid-October.

For general information about the park, contact the Superintendent, 87 North Ripley Street, Isle Royale National Park, Houghton, MI 49931; 906-482-0984. You might want to ask about whatever books, pamphlets, and trail maps are available for sale through the Isle Royale Natural History Association.

For information about lodging at Rock Harbor Lodge, contact National Park Concessions, Inc.: (May to September) P.O. Box 405, Houghton, MI 49931-0405, 906-337-4993; or (October to April) General Offices, Mammoth Cave, KY 42259-0027, 502-773-2191.

Here's the skinny on the boat rides from Michigan: You need to drive a couple hours farther to get to Copper Harbor to take that boat. Then again, the lake crossing is about twenty miles and two hours shorter. Plus, that boat runs daily service during peak tourist times. (The Houghton ferry, *Ranger III*, runs only twice a week.) Crossings are conveniently scheduled for the innkeepers of Copper Harbor. The boat to the island leaves early in the morning; it returns to Copper Harbor in the evening. Unless you want to do a lot of driving on the same day you have your crossings, you'll need to plan for an additional two nights in Copper Harbor.

For information on the *Ranger III* boat operated by the National Park Service, contact the superintendent at the above address in Houghton.

You can book passage from Copper Harbor on the *Isle Royale Queen III* by contacting Isle Royale Ferry Service, P.O. Box 24, Copper Harbor, MI 49918; 906-289-4437 or (off-season) 906-482-4950.

On-demand charter air service to Isle Royale is available through Isle Royale Seaplane Service, Inc., P.O. Box 371, Houghton, MI 49931; 906-482-8850, mid-May to mid-September only.

You can also reach Isle Royale from Minnesota. Contact Grand Portage–Isle Royale Transportation Line, Inc., 1507 North First Street, Superior, WI 54880; 715-392-2100.

ESTIVANT PINES SANCTUARY

If you spend time in Copper Harbor, whether awaiting the boat ride to Isle Royale National Park or as a planned overnight destination on your itinerary, you'll find dozens of attractions clamoring for your attention. Asked to vote for their favorite, residents of Keweenaw County selected Estivant Pines Sanctuary, one of Michigan's last remaining stands of virgin white pines. Additionally, the sanctuary gently nudges visitors toward an understanding of the complex and rugged design features of this part of the state.

Serious lovers of both nature and solitude will appreciate the effort needed in order to arrive at the heart of this sanctuary. The road into the pines is a pretty rough dirt road. Even though it supposedly has been "improved," you'll want to drive with care. Likewise the paths in the sanctuary require that you walk with care. Be sure to wear shoes that offer good support and fairly rigid soles. In addition to being rocky, the trails are also hilly. A hike in the Pines will not be exhausting but will be a little strenuous. Put it like this: Estivant can be considered to be a spur along the Copper Harbor Pathway. A map of the pathway's twenty-five miles of ski loops includes only about a half mile rated as "easy" skiing. The Estivant loop is rated as "more difficult."

Two short loops evolve from the trail leading from the parking area. The Cathedral Loop Trail is 1.5 miles long, the Memorial Loop Trail, 1.4 miles. Combine both, and you will have hiked 2.1 miles. Casual hikers will not want to leave the trail. If you think you've strayed, look for the blue trail markers. If you do want to hike off-trail, be sure to carry a compass and topographic maps for the Fort Wilkins and Lake Medora quadrangles.

What you'll find is a magnificent stand of Eastern white

pines, some of which have been growing for 500 years. Beneath the towering pines, however, expect to find a variety of hardwoods and other conifers such as white cedar, balsam fir, hemlock, and white spruce. A variety of mosses, grasses, ferns, willows, and wildflowers help comprise the listing of 256 plants and trees located within Estivant.

An area so species-rich in flora is likewise rich with fauna. White-tailed deer, black bear, snowshoe rabbits, and a variety of squirrels and chipmunks call the Keweenaw "home." Be prepared to have the bejeebers startled out of you from the dozens of chipmunks who seem to scurry from nowhere in particular whenever you forget about them and let your guard down. Also, in Estivant alone, birders have recorded eighty-seven species of nesting birds. These species include over a dozen types of warblers, several hawk owls, a half-dozen flycatchers, and several thrush types. They range in size from the ruby-throated hummingbird to the red-shouldered hawk.

At the extreme southern end of the sanctuary, a narrow strip leads to the Montreal River and the "Leaning Giant," once Michigan's champion white pine. Standing 120 feet and with a diameter of almost eight feet, the Giant was estimated to be over 500 years old when it was toppled. Man was not the culprit here, though. The tree gave way to a twenty-four-mile-an-hour wind in October 1987.

How to get there: In Keweenaw County, from the end of US 41 in Copper Harbor, turn east (right) and head toward Fort Wilkins State Park for 0.2 of a mile. Turn south (right) onto the road that runs between Lakes Fanny Hooe and Manganese. Follow that road for 2.3 miles. Turn right onto a backcountry dirt road and follow that for .65 of a mile. You'll see some signs indicating the parking area for Estivant Pines.

General information: The trails are designed for foot traffic only — no wheeled or motorized vehicles, no horses. No camping or fires within the sanctuary. Pets must be leashed. Be sure to be properly supplied with bug dope during summer. You can also expect the trails to be wet and slippery, especially in the lower areas near the river.

For more information about Estivant Pines or other area attractions, contact the Keweenaw Tourism Council, 1197 Calumet Avenue, Calumet, MI 49913; 800-338-7982, 906-337-4579, or 906-482-2388.

You can also contact the Keweenaw Peninsula Chamber of Commerce, P.O. Box 336, Houghton, MI 49931; 906-482-5240.

Estivant Pines Sanctuary is one of fourteen sanctuaries owned and administered by the Michigan Nature Association (MNA) on the Keweenaw Peninsula alone. This private, volunteer-intense group has established 140 sanctuaries in a statewide attempt to preserve natural wildlife and protect sensitive species from the steel claws and concrete drool of development.

For the *MNA Sanctuary Guidebook* 7th Ed., send a check or money order for $29.00 to the Michigan Nature Association, P.O. Box 102, Avoca, MI 48006-0102.

You can also order the booklet *Walking Paths in Keweenaw* for $11.00.

PORCUPINE MOUNTAINS WILDERNESS STATE PARK

The Lake of the Clouds Overlook in the Porcupine Mountains Wilderness plants you directly on rock formations that are over a billion years old.

"Kind of makes you feel insignificant, doesn't it," I asked my wife, Maureen.

"It makes me feel young," she chirped and skipped back to the car.

She could do that because she wasn't reeling beneath the additional weight of some other big numbers. The Porcupine

Mountains Wilderness is the largest of all of Michigan's state parks, containing 63,000 acres, over half of which remain virgin forest. The Porkies include ninety-two square miles of wooded hills and ninety miles of wilderness foot trails. Cross-country skiers can enjoy twenty-five miles of groomed trails. Over ninety waterfalls have been identified in the park, but only fourteen have been named. If you're the type of person who needs lots of room to roam, the Porkies were created just for you—a billion years ago, of course.

Such an age requires a geological explanation, and that's just what you get when you visit the interpretive area at the visitors center. A large relief map of the area gives you a bit of an understanding of Mother Nature's handiwork here, as if the land were just wet clay she squeezed, the ridges being the clay that oozed above a couple of her fingers. After taking a look at the map, be sure to watch the brief multiprojector slide show, which adds historical perspective the way the map did with the geological.

The Ojibwa Indians called the area *Kaugabissing*, or "place of the porcupine," after the outline they saw of the escarpment sloping toward the Lake Superior shore. And get this: no fossils are found in these rocks because they are so old they are "pre-life."

The rocks were rich in copper, however, and the first great mining rush in America flowed toward the Porkies in 1841. At one time there were forty-five mines in or near the area that became the park. Loggers followed miners, but Ma Nature, with an indignation you just have to respect, halted their advance. The rugged topography of the Porkies steadfastly refused human overtures, and logging activities were limited to the outer regions of the area. So the interior reaches of the park contain the primary (uncut) timber. This includes 35,000 acres of virgin maple-hemlock forest, the largest such primary stand between the Adirondacks and the Rockies.

Campers will be greeted by a variety of facilities from a modern campground at Union Bay to the most rustic spot where they choose to erect their tents. The Presque Isle River camping area offers semi-modern camping with no electric hookups. Also, rustic cabins containing from two to eight bunks can be reserved. They are situated near scenic points of interest, water, or along the trails that are groomed for cross-country skiing. These cabins can be rented during winter. Three Adirondack shelters are available to backpackers on a first-come, first-served basis. About half a dozen rustic campgrounds are scattered throughout the park. And you really are allowed to put up a tent anywhere along a trail, but not within a quarter mile of any cabin, shelter, scenic area, or road.

In addition to camping and backpacking, the Porkies offer tons of opportunities for birders, rockhounds, photographers, day hikers, and scenery junkies.

"If Bruce and I head for the U.P. in October, do you suggest any place to see the colors?" my sister Mary Ann asked, contemplating her first autumn as a retiree.

Heck Yes!

Here's exactly what I thought after taking the half-mile climb to the forty-foot observation tower at Summit Peak: I will be standing here early some morning during the first October I am retired.

This is another easy-to-get-to feature of the park. In fact, it seems that the DNR built roads and short trails to those features that attract most people, thus making it easier for more people to visit. So if you don't like the idea of rubbing elbows with strangers when you head out, try hitting the trail early in the morning.

The half-mile hiking trail to Summit Peak is well maintained but steep. At 1,958 feet, Summit Peak is the highest spot in the Porkies. From there you can look down on the surrounding peaks, miles of forest, Lake Superior, the Apostle Islands, and

Isle Royale on a good day. Be sure to take along good binoculars with you so you can tell if you're looking at a recreational sailboat or a freighter on the bounding main.

Several other overlooks are accessible via hikes and are marked on the area map you can pick up at the visitors center.

Pine martens are such agile climbers they feed on squirrels

So too are about half a dozen waterfalls. But if you're going to visit only one, make it the Presque Isle Falls.

Actually, you'll see three for the price of one at this western end of park. A short, quarter-mile walk from the parking area brings you to the boardwalk that gets you to the three falls named after Ojibwa *manitous* or "spirit warriors": *Manido*, *Nawadaha*, and the largest of the falls, *Manabezho*. Make sure you cross the suspension bridge to view from another angle the river that was rated among the "Top Ten" in North America.

People interested in flora will find over 200 species of plants and trees, more notably the nodding trillium, pitcher plant, pink and yellow lady's slipper, large trillium, Michigan lily, and Scottish bluebells. Look carefully along the escarpment in mid-May for the short-lived Collinsia, whose primary range is the Rocky Mountains.

Fauna lovers will appreciate the diversity of the more than 150 species of birds sighted at various times in the Porkies, the most special of which have been peregrine falcons, which started showing up in the area in 1990. They're thought to have come from the releases at Bergland about twenty miles away. Both bald and golden eagles have been spotted in the park.

As far as mammals go, yes, you can see porcupines in the Porkies. You may see a bear. The fisher and pine marten, both solitary animals who survive best in the canopy of old-growth timber, are doing well since they were reintroduced to the area in the 1960s. Gray wolves have been seen in the area, as have some moose, but you shouldn't base a trip to the Porkies on the hope of seeing either species. You may, however, see white-tailed deer feeding along roads at dusk. Drive carefully.

Finally, the Porkies are known as a gem of an alpine ski area. Nestled as they are so far from the glorified ski locales, the Porkies offer a degree of serenity and solitude that you won't find at the big-name ski lodges. The hill has a vertical drop of 600 feet, with the longest run being 6,000 feet. The ten miles of alpine ski runs include three novice trails, seven intermediate, and three expert.

Nordic skiers and snowshoers who desire the ultimate winter survival challenge will be happy to learn that they can get permits for backcountry camping in the wintertime.

You should know, however, that South Boundary Road is plowed only through the end of November. And M-107 is kept open only as far as the ski area.

How to get there: From M-28 travel north on M-64 about eighteen miles to Silver City (in Ontonagon County). Turn left onto M-107 and follow the signs to the visitors center.

General information: A state parks motor vehicle permit is required for entry.

Backpackers must register at the visitors center. They must be prepared to bury human waste and tissue paper and to pack out noncombustible waste. No fires are allowed except in designated fire rings. The DNR advises you to use a pack stove for cooking.

Remember to hang your food cache so the bears can't get to it, and don't eat or prepare food inside your tent. And be sure to bring plenty of bug spray if you visit between late May and mid-July.

For reservations and general information about the park, contact the Park Manager, Porcupine Mountains State Park, 599 M-107, Ontonagon, MI 49953; 906-885-5275.

An excellent, helpful text about this remarkable area of Michigan has been produced by two state park rangers, Michael Rafferty and Robert Sprague. *Porcupine Mountains Companion* (2d edition) is available from the gift shop at the visitors center. "Companion" is a fine name for this book, for in addition to relying on its advice as you plan your trip, you're going to want to carry it along during your visit. It provides historical and geological explanations, highlights of each of the trails you might hike, recommended waterfalls hikes, and more. Ask for ordering information when you contact the park manager at the above address.

SYLVANIA RECREATION AREA

Silence.

If you're lucky, the pure, natural, deafening silence of nature is the first feature to greet you as you step from your car into the Sylvania wilderness, an excellent overnight destination if you want to enjoy the solitude of a backcountry canoe/camp trip.

Silence surrounds you when you register for your campsite, as you prepare to launch your canoe, as you slip into the calm waters of Clark Lake.

As you paddle, few sounds interrupt the gurgle of the water on the bow of the canoe. Perhaps the wind. Or some black squirrels chattering away in the trees a quarter mile away. The utter silence is pierced only by the water dribbling from your paddle as you take a break.

If you're lucky, other human visitors will likewise respect the quiet as you paddle to the southeastern shore of Clark Lake. From there, you'll want to take one of three possible portages into other waters. Since a portage requires some effort, sightings of other humans dwindle once you get on one of these secondary bodies of water.

As you relax at your campsite, the water lapping the shore is the loudest distraction. Except for the loons, of course. But then again, the chants of these shamans of the wilderness are an enhancement, not a distraction.

Consider the Sylvania Tract Michigan's equivalent of the Boundary Waters Canoe Area (BWCA) in Minnesota, with some differences. Sylvania is nowhere near the size of the BWCA, neither on the grand scale nor in its individual features of water and land.

Perhaps the main difference lies in the effect each area has on your psyche. In the BWCA, nature simply overwhelms, over-powers with her awesome display of majesty and her formidable countenance, and you simply acquiesce. In Sylvania, however, she subdues that aspect ever so slightly beneath the surface, teas-ing you with the thought that she remains placid, welcoming, all-embracing.

For example, from my camp on Loon Lake, I noticed that the morning's skies were fiercely gray. Paddling the solo canoe as fiercely as I could, I hugged the west shoreline, keeping out of the west winds as best I could. By the time I reached Clark Lake, the winds had died a bit, but the skies still threatened. At Mar-quette, 100 miles away, these same winds capsized a small motorboat, killing two fishermen. In the midst of this mood that chased me from her bosom, Nature quickly changed and showed another side.

A small loon, old enough to swim on its own and not hitch a ride on Mama's back, started crying, almost whimpering. I quit paddling and watched. It just kept crying while swimming in a big circle. It even poked its head beneath the surface to take a look. Then, about thirty yards away, an adult loon, presumably its mother, popped to the surface. The happy little loon skittered to her side. A tender moment nature had decided to share.

The Sylvania Recreation Area is practically paradise for people who enjoy self-propelled, nonmechanized transportation. It contains 21,000 acres, 4,000 of which are water. Motorboats are allowed only on two lakes, Crooked and Long. Vehicle travel is limited to the roads on the outskirts of the area. No wheeled vehicles are allowed in the interior at all—this includes bicycles and carts used to transport boats or canoes. No snowmobiles are allowed, but the opportunities for cross-country skiing are unlimited.

Nordic skiers will use the same twenty-six miles of trails that are open to hikers and backpackers. In fact, the eighty-four wilderness campsites can be reached by hiking as well as by water. There's also a forty-eight-unit campground with auto access. This campground has water available, while the others don't. So if you hike or canoe more than a day away from your vehicle, you must remain self-sufficient.

The usual array of Michigan mammals may be encountered here: white-tailed deer, racoon, beaver, otter, coyote, fox, mink, and others. Also, this is black bear country, so you need to take special precautions with your food cache.

In addition to the loons you might encounter, be on the lookout for bald eagles. (Remember, in Michigan, the adult bald eagle is the only bird you'll see that has a white head and white tail.)

How to get there: In Gogebic County, the Sylvania visitors center is located near the town of Watersmeet along US 2 on a hill just east of its junction with US 45. To arrive at one entry point, continue west on US 2 for four miles to County 535. Follow 535 southwest for about four miles and watch for the signs leading to the boat access on Clark Lake.

General information: The crystal clear condition of the water in Sylvania may tempt you to drink straight from the lakes, but the U.S. Forest Service advises against that. You should either boil water for five minutes or filter it and treat it with devices or chemicals designed to remove or kill the *Giardia lamblia* parasites.

The crystal waters may also invite you to try to catch some fish. Special fishing regulations have been established for the Sylvania Wilderness. Be sure to request a card that explains them.

May and June are the worst mosquito and blackfly months. Don't forget that bug dope!

A maximum of five people are allowed per wilderness campsite, and the group size for any purpose is limited to ten.

Budget restrictions have forced changes in the campsite

reservation and registration process. It's best to contact the visitors center directly for up-to-date information. Registrations were being taken from January 15 to May 15.

Also, in an attempt to protect the fragile nature of this wilderness, several other regulations are in effect and several other suggestions and requests are made of visitors. Such specifics are available from the visitors center when you contact it for reservation information. To do so, write Sylvania Wilderness Permits, Watersmeet Visitor Center, P.O. Box 276, Watersmeet, MI 49969; 906-358-4724 or 4834. From February 1 to May 14, call Monday through Friday between 10:00 A.M. and 4:00 P.M., CST. From May 15 to September 30, you can call seven days a week from 7:30 A.M. to 5:00 P.M. CST.

You can also request other Sylvania information from the Watersmeet Ranger Station, Watersmeet, MI 49969; 906-358-4551.

For information on canoe rentals in the area, contact the Chamber of Commerce, P.O. Box 36, Watersmeet, MI 49969; 906-358-4569.

KITCH-ITI-KIPI (BIG SPRINGS)

Kitch-iti-kipi is Michigan's largest spring—200 feet across, 40 feet deep, with a year-round, continuous flow of 16,000 gallons a minute of 45-degree water. According to one Ojibwa legend, the spring was named after a young Ojibwa chieftain who died in its icy waters as he tried to prove himself to his girlfriend.

From a moving observation platform, visitors can peer into the crystal depths and see the floor of the spring "erupt" when water bubbles up through it. They'll also see massive brown trout idly swimming about. The observation raft is powered by an "armstrong" engine. That means you have to use your arms to pull the raft along cables which cross over special formations and features of the springs.

How to get there: At the blinking light in Thompson, turn north from US 2 onto M-134. Follow the signs and this road for eleven miles to the entrance to Palm Book State Park.

General information: You'll find a picnic area and concession but no camping at this park. Modern camping, mini-cabins and rent-a-tents are available at nearby Indian Lake State Park. A motor vehicle permit is required for entry to both state parks.

For more information, write to Park Manager, Indian Lake State Park, Route 2, P.O. Box 2500, Manistique, MI 49854; 906-341-2355.

You can also contact the Schoolcraft County Chamber of Commerce, P.O. Box 72, Manistique, MI 49854; 906-341-5010.

Appendix

1. Free highway maps of the state and travel publications are available from Michigan Travel Bureau, P.O. Box 30225, Lansing, MI 48909; 800-543-2937.

2. The best maps of the five-county Detroit Metropolitan area are available free from Huron-Clinton Metropolitan Authority, 13000 High Ridge Drive, P. O. Box 2001, Brighton, MI 48116-8001; 800-477-2757.

3. An index of topographic maps of the state can be ordered free from the Michigan United Conservation Club Map Center, P.O. Box 30235, Lansing, MI 48909; 800-777-6720.

4. U.S. Forest Service wilderness and recreation areas and National Scenic Trail

- *Western Upper Peninsula:* Ottawa National Forest, East US 2, Ironwood, MI 49938; 800-562-1201 or 906-932-1330.

- *Central and eastern portions of the Upper Peninsula:* Hiawatha National Forest, 2727 North Lincoln Road, Escanaba, MI 49829; 906-786-4062.

- *Northern Lower Peninsula:* Huron-Manistee National

Forest, 421 South Mitchell Street, Cadillac, MI 49601; 616-775-2421 or 800-821-6263.

- *North Country National Scenic Trail:* National Park Service, P.O. Box 5463, Madison, WI 53705-0463.

5. Michigan Department of Natural Resources
  - For lists of state forest campgrounds and hiking trails/pathways: Forest Management Division, Recreation and Trails Section, P.O. Box 30452, Lansing, MI 48909; 517-373-4175, FAX 517-373-2443.
  - For lists of state parks and information on renting rustic or mini-cabins: Parks and Recreation Division, P.O. Box 30257, Lansing, MI 48909; 517-373-9900 or TDD (for the deaf): 517-335-4623.
  - For information on special species of wildlife such as the Kirtland's warbler, trumpeter swan, Great Lakes piping plover, gray wolf as well as a wildflower viewing guide and a pamphlet outlining Michigan's wilderness and natural areas: Wildlife Division, P.O. Box 30028, Lansing, MI 48909; 517-373-1263.
  - For information on the North Country Trail on state land plus general questions: Information Service Center, P.O. Box 30028, Lansing, MI 48909; 517-373-1220.
  - Maps and information about Michigan's Natural Rivers Program: Land and Water Management Division, Box 30028, Lansing, MI 48909; 517-373-1170.

6. Travel Bureau, Michigan Department of Commerce, P.O. Box 30226, Lansing, MI 48909; 800-543-2937 or TDD: 800-722-8191.

7. Private groups with sanctuaries/preserves open to the public:
  - Michigan Audubon Society, 6011 West St. Joseph, Suite 403, P.O. Box 80527, Lansing, MI 48908-0527; 517-886-9144.
  - Michigan Nature Association, P.O. Box 102, Avoca, MI 48006-0102; 810-324-2626.

- Little Traverse Conservancy, Inc., 3264 Powell Road, Harbor Springs, MI 49740; 616-347-0991.

Recommended Guides

Michigan Atlas & Gazetteer (ISBN 0-89933-221-8), DeLorme Mapping Company, P.O. Box 298, Freeport, ME 04032; 800-452-5931 for nearest dealer or ordering information.

Canoeing Michigan's Rivers (ISBN 0-9608588-4-9) by Jerry Dennis and Craig Date; *A Guide to 199 Michigan Waterfalls* (ISBN 0-9608588-7-3) by The Penrose Family; each is $15.95 ppd. from Friede Publications, 2339 Venezia Drive, Davison, MI 48423.; 800-824-4618.

Field Guide to Great Lakes Coastal Plants (ISBN 1-56525-008-7) by Walter J. Hoagman; $7.95, check payable to Michigan State University; send to Michigan Sea Grant Extension, 334 Natural Resources Building, Michigan State University, East Lansing, MI 48824-1222.

Michigan Wildlife Viewing Guide (due early 1995). Call Department of Natural Resources Natural Heritage Program for pricing and availability, 517-373-1263.

Index

Titles in the Natural Wonders/Green Guide series:

Natural Wonders of Alaska
Natural Wonders of Connecticut & Rhode Island
Natural Wonders of Florida
Green Guide to Hawaii
Natural Wonders of Idaho
Natural Wonders of Massachusetts
Natural Wonders of Michigan
Natural Wonders of New Hampshire
Natural Wonders of New Jersey
Natural Wonders of New York
Natural Wonders of Ohio
Green Guide to Oregon
Natural Wonders of Southern California
Natural Wonders of Texas
Natural Wonders of Vermont
Natural Wonders of Virginia
Green Guide to Washington
Natural Wonders of Wisconsin

All books are $9.95 at bookstores.
Or order directly from the publisher (add $3.00 shipping and
handling for direct orders):

Country Roads Press
P.O. Box 286
Castine, Maine 04421
Toll-free phone number: **800-729-9179**